50 Australian Breakfast Food Recipes for Home

By: Kelly Johnson

Table of Contents

- Classic Vegemite Toast
- Smashed Avocado on Toast with Poached Eggs
- Australian Brekkie Bowl
- Lamington Pancakes
- Barbecue Bacon and Eggs
- Anzac Biscuit Porridge
- Smoked Salmon and Dill Scramble
- Pavlova Fruit Parfait
- Bush Tomato Frittata
- Macadamia Nut Granola
- Kangaroo Sausage Roll
- Flat White Crepes
- Golden Gaytime Waffles
- Beetroot and Goat Cheese Salad
- Blueberry Damper
- Spinach and Cheese Pie
- Pumpkin Scone with Jam
- Tim Tam Banana Bread
- Fairy Bread Pancakes
- Crocodile Crepes
- Emu Poached Eggs
- Sausage Roll Pancakes
- Damper with Jam and Cream
- Anzac Biscuit Muffins
- Kangaroo Stuffed Mushrooms
- Tim Tam Crepes
- Vegemite and Cheese Pie
- Lamington Crepes
- Barbecue Chicken Toast
- Pavlova Toast
- Barbecue Bacon Pancakes
- Barbecue Chicken Pancakes
- Anzac Biscuit Pancakes
- Anzac Biscuit Toast
- Pavlova Pancakes

- Anzac Biscuit Waffles
- Kangaroo Sausage Roll
- Pavlova Waffles
- Pineapple and Coconut Smoothie Bowl
- Chia Seed Pudding with Berries
- Acai Bowl with Granola
- Grilled Veggie Breakfast Wrap
- Caramelized Banana Pancakes
- Australian Meat Pie
- Healthy Breakfast Burrito
- Kiwi and Mango Smoothie
- Barramundi Breakfast Tacos
- Ricotta Hotcakes with Honeycomb Butter
- Avocado and Smoked Trout Bruschetta
- Dukkah Eggs with Spiced Yogurt

Classic Vegemite Toast

Classic Vegemite Toast

Ingredients:

- 2 slices of your favorite bread (such as white, whole wheat, or sourdough)
- Butter or margarine, softened
- Vegemite

Instructions:

1. **Toast the Bread:**
   - Toast the slices of bread to your desired level of crispiness.
2. **Spread Butter:**
   - While the toast is still warm, spread a thin layer of butter or margarine evenly over each slice. This helps balance out the saltiness of the Vegemite.
3. **Apply Vegemite:**
   - Using a butter knife, spread a thin layer of Vegemite over the buttered toast. Start with a small amount and adjust according to your preference. Vegemite is quite salty, so a little goes a long way.
4. **Serve:**
   - Serve the Vegemite toast immediately while the toast is warm and the Vegemite is slightly melted into the butter.

Tips:

- **Adjust Vegemite Amount:** Start with a small amount of Vegemite, especially if you're trying it for the first time. You can always add more if you prefer a stronger flavor.
- **Pairing Suggestions:** Vegemite toast pairs well with a cup of tea or coffee for a classic Australian breakfast experience.
- **Variations:** For a twist, you can add sliced avocado or a poached egg on top of your Vegemite toast to create a more substantial meal.

Vegemite toast is a quick and easy breakfast option that's loved by many Australians for its distinctive flavor. It's a great way to start your day with a taste of Down Under!

Smashed Avocado on Toast with Poached Eggs

Ingredients:

- 2 ripe avocados
- Juice of 1/2 lemon
- Salt and pepper, to taste
- 4 slices of your favorite bread (such as sourdough, whole wheat, or multigrain)
- 4 large eggs
- Vinegar (for poaching eggs)
- Optional toppings: cherry tomatoes, feta cheese, red pepper flakes, or fresh herbs

Instructions:

1. **Prepare the Avocado Smash:**
    - Cut the avocados in half and remove the pits. Scoop the flesh into a bowl.
    - Add the lemon juice, salt, and pepper to the avocado.
    - Use a fork to mash the avocado until smooth or slightly chunky, depending on your preference. Taste and adjust seasoning if needed.
2. **Toast the Bread:**
    - Toast the slices of bread to your desired level of crispiness.
3. **Poach the Eggs:**
    - Fill a large saucepan with water and bring it to a boil. Reduce the heat to a gentle simmer and add a splash of vinegar (about 1 tablespoon) to the water.
    - Crack each egg into a small bowl or ramekin.
    - Create a gentle whirlpool in the simmering water using a spoon and carefully slide the eggs, one at a time, into the center of the whirlpool. This helps the egg whites wrap around the yolks.
    - Cook the eggs for about 3-4 minutes for a soft poach or longer for a firmer yolk. Remove the poached eggs with a slotted spoon and drain on a paper towel.
4. **Assemble the Dish:**
    - Spread a generous amount of smashed avocado onto each slice of toasted bread.
    - Carefully place a poached egg on top of each avocado toast.
5. **Add Optional Toppings:**
    - Sprinkle with additional salt and pepper if desired.
    - Add optional toppings such as halved cherry tomatoes, crumbled feta cheese, red pepper flakes, or fresh herbs like chopped parsley or cilantro.

6. **Serve Immediately:**
    - Serve the smashed avocado on toast with poached eggs immediately, while the eggs are warm and the avocado is fresh.

Tips:

- **Ripe Avocados:** Use ripe avocados that yield slightly to gentle pressure when squeezed. They should be creamy and easy to mash.
- **Poaching Eggs:** For a perfect poach, ensure the water is at a gentle simmer and use fresh eggs for better results.
- **Variations:** Customize your smashed avocado toast with additional toppings such as crispy bacon, smoked salmon, or a drizzle of hot sauce for extra flavor.

Smashed avocado on toast with poached eggs is a nutritious and satisfying breakfast or brunch option that combines creamy avocado with the richness of a perfectly poached egg. Enjoy this flavorful dish to start your day on a delicious note!

Australian Brekkie Bowl

Ingredients:

- 1 cup cooked quinoa or brown rice
- 1 avocado, sliced or mashed
- 2 eggs, poached or fried
- 1 cup baby spinach leaves
- 1/2 cup cherry tomatoes, halved
- 1/4 cup canned chickpeas, rinsed and drained
- 1/4 cup feta cheese, crumbled
- Salt and pepper, to taste
- Optional toppings: sliced cucumber, roasted sweet potatoes, pumpkin seeds, fresh herbs (such as parsley or basil)

Instructions:

1. **Prepare the Base:**
    - Cook quinoa or brown rice according to package instructions until tender. Fluff with a fork and set aside.
2. **Cook the Eggs:**
    - Poach or fry the eggs to your liking. For poached eggs, follow the poaching instructions from the previous recipe.
3. **Assemble the Brekkie Bowl:**
    - Divide the cooked quinoa or brown rice evenly among serving bowls.
    - Arrange sliced avocado, baby spinach leaves, cherry tomatoes, and chickpeas around the bowl.
4. **Add Eggs and Toppings:**
    - Place the poached or fried eggs on top of the bowl.
    - Sprinkle with crumbled feta cheese and season with salt and pepper to taste.
5. **Garnish and Serve:**
    - Garnish the brekkie bowl with optional toppings such as sliced cucumber, roasted sweet potatoes, pumpkin seeds, and fresh herbs.
6. **Enjoy Immediately:**
    - Serve the Australian Brekkie Bowl immediately while warm. Mix all the ingredients together or enjoy them separately, as desired.

Tips:

- **Variations:** Feel free to customize your brekkie bowl with other ingredients such as smoked salmon, grilled chicken, or roasted vegetables.
- **Make-Ahead:** You can cook the quinoa or brown rice and prepare the ingredients in advance for a quick assembly in the morning.
- **Dietary Modifications:** Make it vegan by omitting the eggs and feta cheese, and adding plant-based protein such as tofu or tempeh.

The Australian Brekkie Bowl is a versatile dish that allows you to incorporate your favorite ingredients while providing a nutritious and satisfying breakfast. It's perfect for starting your day with energy and flavor!

Lamington Pancakes

Ingredients:

For the Pancakes:

- 1 cup all-purpose flour
- 2 tablespoons granulated sugar
- 1 teaspoon baking powder
- 1/2 teaspoon baking soda
- Pinch of salt
- 1 cup buttermilk (or 1 cup milk + 1 tablespoon vinegar or lemon juice)
- 1 large egg
- 2 tablespoons unsalted butter, melted
- 1 teaspoon vanilla extract

For the Chocolate Sauce:

- 1/2 cup unsweetened cocoa powder
- 1/2 cup powdered sugar
- 1/2 cup milk
- 1/2 teaspoon vanilla extract

For Coating:

- 1 cup shredded coconut (desiccated coconut)

Instructions:

1. **Prepare the Chocolate Sauce:**
    - In a small saucepan, combine cocoa powder, powdered sugar, milk, and vanilla extract.
    - Heat over medium-low heat, stirring constantly, until smooth and slightly thickened. Remove from heat and set aside.
2. **Make the Pancakes:**
    - In a large bowl, whisk together flour, sugar, baking powder, baking soda, and salt.
    - In another bowl, whisk together buttermilk (or milk + vinegar/lemon juice), egg, melted butter, and vanilla extract.
    - Pour the wet ingredients into the dry ingredients and stir until just combined. Do not overmix; a few lumps are okay.

- Heat a non-stick skillet or griddle over medium heat and lightly grease with butter or oil.
- Pour about 1/4 cup of batter onto the skillet for each pancake. Cook until bubbles form on the surface and the edges look set, about 2-3 minutes. Flip and cook for another 1-2 minutes until golden brown and cooked through.
- Transfer cooked pancakes to a plate and cover with a clean kitchen towel to keep warm.

3. **Assemble the Lamington Pancakes:**
    - Spread shredded coconut on a plate.
    - Take each pancake and dip it into the chocolate sauce, coating both sides generously.
    - Immediately roll the chocolate-covered pancake in shredded coconut, ensuring it sticks to the chocolate sauce.
    - Repeat with remaining pancakes.

4. **Serve:**
    - Arrange Lamington Pancakes on a serving platter and drizzle with any remaining chocolate sauce.
    - Serve warm and enjoy the delicious combination of fluffy pancakes, rich chocolate sauce, and coconut!

Tips:

- **Freshness:** Lamington Pancakes are best enjoyed fresh. If you have leftovers, store them in an airtight container in the refrigerator and reheat gently before serving.
- **Variations:** For added texture and flavor, you can add a layer of whipped cream or mascarpone cheese between the pancakes before coating with chocolate and coconut.

Lamington Pancakes offer a delightful twist on the classic Australian treat, combining the beloved flavors of lamingtons with fluffy pancakes. They're perfect for a special breakfast or brunch that will impress your family and friends!

Barbecue Bacon and Eggs

Ingredients:

- 4 slices bacon
- 4 large eggs
- 1/4 cup barbecue sauce (your favorite variety)
- Salt and pepper, to taste
- Fresh chives or parsley, chopped (for garnish, optional)

Instructions:

1. **Cook the Bacon:**
   - In a skillet over medium heat, cook the bacon slices until crispy. Remove the bacon from the skillet and drain on a paper towel-lined plate. Set aside.
2. **Prepare the Eggs:**
   - In the same skillet with the bacon drippings, crack the eggs carefully to keep the yolks intact.
   - Cook the eggs over medium heat until the whites are set but the yolks are still runny, or to your desired doneness.
   - Season the eggs with salt and pepper to taste.
3. **Add Barbecue Sauce:**
   - Once the eggs are nearly cooked, drizzle barbecue sauce over each egg. Allow the sauce to warm through for about 1 minute.
4. **Assemble:**
   - Place a slice of cooked bacon on each plate.
   - Carefully transfer the barbecue eggs onto the bacon slices.
5. **Garnish and Serve:**
   - Garnish with chopped fresh chives or parsley, if desired.
   - Serve immediately while warm, with toast or your favorite breakfast sides.

Tips:

- **Barbecue Sauce Variation:** Choose your favorite barbecue sauce for this recipe. Whether sweet, smoky, or spicy, the sauce will add depth and flavor to the dish.
- **Bacon Crisping:** For crispier bacon, cook it until it reaches your desired level of crispiness before adding the eggs to the skillet.
- **Presentation:** Arrange the barbecue bacon and eggs on individual plates for a visually appealing breakfast presentation.

Barbecue bacon and eggs is a satisfying breakfast option that combines the smokiness of bacon with the richness of eggs and the tangy sweetness of barbecue sauce. It's perfect for a weekend brunch or any day you want to start with a hearty and flavorful meal!

Anzac Biscuit Porridge

Ingredients:

- 1 cup rolled oats
- 2 cups milk (dairy or plant-based)
- 2 tablespoons golden syrup or honey
- 1 tablespoon butter
- 1/4 cup desiccated coconut
- 1/4 cup brown sugar
- 1/4 cup chopped almonds or pecans
- 1/2 teaspoon vanilla extract
- Pinch of salt
- Optional toppings: extra golden syrup, sliced bananas, berries, or additional coconut for garnish

Instructions:

1. **Toast the Oats:**
   - In a dry saucepan over medium heat, toast the rolled oats for 3-4 minutes, stirring frequently, until fragrant and lightly golden. Remove from heat and set aside.
2. **Prepare the Anzac Biscuit Mixture:**
   - In the same saucepan, melt the butter over medium heat.
   - Add desiccated coconut, brown sugar, and chopped almonds or pecans. Cook, stirring constantly, for 1-2 minutes until the mixture is fragrant and the sugar begins to dissolve.
3. **Cook the Porridge:**
   - Pour in the milk and add the toasted oats to the saucepan.
   - Stir in golden syrup or honey, vanilla extract, and a pinch of salt.
   - Bring the mixture to a simmer over medium heat, then reduce the heat to low.
   - Cook, stirring occasionally, for 5-7 minutes or until the oats are tender and the porridge has thickened to your desired consistency.
4. **Serve:**
   - Remove the Anzac Biscuit Porridge from heat and divide it into serving bowls.
   - Drizzle with extra golden syrup, if desired, and garnish with sliced bananas, berries, or additional coconut.

Tips:

- **Texture Variation:** For a creamier porridge, use more milk or add a splash of cream during cooking.
- **Make-Ahead:** Prepare a larger batch of Anzac Biscuit Porridge and store leftovers in the refrigerator. Reheat gently with a splash of milk or water before serving.
- **Nut-Free Option:** If you have nut allergies, omit the almonds or pecans and substitute with seeds such as sunflower seeds or pumpkin seeds.

Anzac Biscuit Porridge is a delightful twist on classic oatmeal, incorporating the flavors of Anzac biscuits into a warm and comforting breakfast. It's a perfect choice for chilly mornings or anytime you crave a cozy and flavorful start to your day!

Anzac Biscuit Porridge

Ingredients:

- 1 cup rolled oats
- 2 cups milk (dairy or plant-based)
- 2 tablespoons golden syrup or honey
- 1 tablespoon butter
- 1/4 cup desiccated coconut
- 1/4 cup brown sugar
- 1/4 cup chopped almonds or pecans
- 1/2 teaspoon vanilla extract
- Pinch of salt
- Optional toppings: extra golden syrup, sliced bananas, berries, or additional coconut for garnish

Instructions:

1. **Toast the Oats:**
    - In a dry saucepan over medium heat, toast the rolled oats for 3-4 minutes, stirring frequently, until fragrant and lightly golden. Remove from heat and set aside.
2. **Prepare the Anzac Biscuit Mixture:**
    - In the same saucepan, melt the butter over medium heat.
    - Add desiccated coconut, brown sugar, and chopped almonds or pecans. Cook, stirring constantly, for 1-2 minutes until the mixture is fragrant and the sugar begins to dissolve.
3. **Cook the Porridge:**
    - Pour in the milk and add the toasted oats to the saucepan.
    - Stir in golden syrup or honey, vanilla extract, and a pinch of salt.
    - Bring the mixture to a simmer over medium heat, then reduce the heat to low.
    - Cook, stirring occasionally, for 5-7 minutes or until the oats are tender and the porridge has thickened to your desired consistency.
4. **Serve:**
    - Remove the Anzac Biscuit Porridge from heat and divide it into serving bowls.
    - Drizzle with extra golden syrup, if desired, and garnish with sliced bananas, berries, or additional coconut.

Tips:

- **Texture Variation:** For a creamier porridge, use more milk or add a splash of cream during cooking.
- **Make-Ahead:** Prepare a larger batch of Anzac Biscuit Porridge and store leftovers in the refrigerator. Reheat gently with a splash of milk or water before serving.
- **Nut-Free Option:** If you have nut allergies, omit the almonds or pecans and substitute with seeds such as sunflower seeds or pumpkin seeds.

Anzac Biscuit Porridge is a delightful twist on classic oatmeal, incorporating the flavors of Anzac biscuits into a warm and comforting breakfast. It's a perfect choice for chilly mornings or anytime you crave a cozy and flavorful start to your day!

Smoked Salmon and Dill Scramble

Ingredients:

- 4 large eggs
- 2 tablespoons milk or cream
- Salt and pepper, to taste
- 1 tablespoon butter
- 100g smoked salmon, thinly sliced
- 2 tablespoons fresh dill, chopped
- Optional garnish: additional fresh dill, lemon wedges

Instructions:

1. **Prepare the Eggs:**
    - In a bowl, whisk together eggs, milk or cream, salt, and pepper until well combined.
2. **Cook the Eggs:**
    - Heat a non-stick skillet over medium heat and add the butter. Allow the butter to melt and coat the pan evenly.
    - Pour the egg mixture into the skillet and let it cook undisturbed for a few seconds until the edges start to set.
    - Gently stir the eggs with a spatula, pushing them from the edges toward the center. Continue to cook, stirring occasionally, until the eggs are mostly set but still slightly creamy.
3. **Add Smoked Salmon and Dill:**
    - Add the smoked salmon slices to the eggs and continue to gently fold them in until the salmon is heated through and the eggs are cooked to your desired consistency.
4. **Finish and Serve:**
    - Remove the skillet from heat and sprinkle chopped fresh dill over the scrambled eggs. Stir gently to incorporate the dill.
    - Transfer the Smoked Salmon and Dill Scramble to serving plates or bowls.
    - Garnish with additional fresh dill and lemon wedges, if desired.
    - Serve immediately while warm, accompanied by toast or your favorite breakfast sides.

Tips:

- **Creaminess:** For creamier scrambled eggs, add a little more milk or cream to the egg mixture before cooking.
- **Variations:** Incorporate chopped chives or green onions for added flavor and color.
- **Presentation:** Serve Smoked Salmon and Dill Scramble on toasted bagels or English muffins for a classic brunch option.

Smoked Salmon and Dill Scramble is a delightful breakfast option that's both flavorful and satisfying. It's perfect for special occasions or leisurely weekend mornings when you want to enjoy a luxurious breakfast treat.

Pavlova Fruit Parfait

Ingredients:

- 4 small store-bought meringue nests or homemade meringues, crushed
- 1 cup Greek yogurt or whipped cream
- 1 tablespoon powdered sugar (optional, adjust to taste)
- 1 teaspoon vanilla extract
- 1 cup mixed fresh fruits (such as strawberries, blueberries, kiwi, mango, etc.), chopped or sliced
- Fresh mint leaves, for garnish (optional)

Instructions:

1. **Prepare the Yogurt or Whipped Cream:**
    - If using Greek yogurt, mix it with powdered sugar (if desired) and vanilla extract until well combined. If using whipped cream, whip it until soft peaks form.
2. **Prepare the Fruits:**
    - Wash, peel (if necessary), and chop or slice the fresh fruits into bite-sized pieces.
3. **Assemble the Parfaits:**
    - In serving glasses or bowls, layer crushed meringue at the bottom.
    - Add a layer of Greek yogurt or whipped cream on top of the meringue.
    - Add a layer of mixed fresh fruits on top of the yogurt or whipped cream.
    - Repeat the layers until the glasses or bowls are filled, ending with a layer of fresh fruits on top.
4. **Garnish:**
    - Garnish with fresh mint leaves for a pop of color and freshness.
5. **Serve:**
    - Serve immediately as a refreshing dessert or breakfast treat.

Tips:

- **Make-Ahead:** You can prepare the crushed meringue, yogurt or whipped cream, and chopped fruits ahead of time and assemble the parfaits just before serving to keep them fresh and crispy.
- **Variations:** Experiment with different combinations of fruits and flavors. You can also drizzle a little honey or fruit compote between the layers for added sweetness.

- **Presentation:** Serve Pavlova Fruit Parfaits in clear glasses or jars to showcase the beautiful layers.

Pavlova Fruit Parfait is a delightful dessert that combines the lightness of meringue with the creaminess of yogurt or whipped cream and the freshness of seasonal fruits. It's a perfect choice for a refreshing and elegant treat, whether as a dessert after a meal or as a light and satisfying snack. Enjoy the contrast of textures and flavors in every spoonful!

Bush Tomato Frittata

Ingredients:

- 4 small store-bought meringue nests or homemade meringues, crushed
- 1 cup Greek yogurt or whipped cream
- 1 tablespoon powdered sugar (optional, adjust to taste)
- 1 teaspoon vanilla extract
- 1 cup mixed fresh fruits (such as strawberries, blueberries, kiwi, mango, etc.), chopped or sliced
- Fresh mint leaves, for garnish (optional)

Instructions:

1. **Prepare the Yogurt or Whipped Cream:**
    - If using Greek yogurt, mix it with powdered sugar (if desired) and vanilla extract until well combined. If using whipped cream, whip it until soft peaks form.
2. **Prepare the Fruits:**
    - Wash, peel (if necessary), and chop or slice the fresh fruits into bite-sized pieces.
3. **Assemble the Parfaits:**
    - In serving glasses or bowls, layer crushed meringue at the bottom.
    - Add a layer of Greek yogurt or whipped cream on top of the meringue.
    - Add a layer of mixed fresh fruits on top of the yogurt or whipped cream.
    - Repeat the layers until the glasses or bowls are filled, ending with a layer of fresh fruits on top.
4. **Garnish:**
    - Garnish with fresh mint leaves for a pop of color and freshness.
5. **Serve:**
    - Serve immediately as a refreshing dessert or breakfast treat.

Tips:

- **Make-Ahead:** You can prepare the crushed meringue, yogurt or whipped cream, and chopped fruits ahead of time and assemble the parfaits just before serving to keep them fresh and crispy.
- **Variations:** Experiment with different combinations of fruits and flavors. You can also drizzle a little honey or fruit compote between the layers for added sweetness.

- **Presentation:** Serve Pavlova Fruit Parfaits in clear glasses or jars to showcase the beautiful layers.

Pavlova Fruit Parfait is a delightful dessert that combines the lightness of meringue with the creaminess of yogurt or whipped cream and the freshness of seasonal fruits. It's a perfect choice for a refreshing and elegant treat, whether as a dessert after a meal or as a light and satisfying snack. Enjoy the contrast of textures and flavors in every spoonful!

Bush Tomato Frittata

Ingredients:

- 6 large eggs
- 1/4 cup milk or cream
- 1/4 teaspoon salt
- 1/4 teaspoon black pepper
- 1 tablespoon olive oil
- 1 small onion, finely chopped
- 1 clove garlic, minced
- 1/2 cup sun-dried tomatoes (preferably bush tomatoes), chopped
- 1/2 cup baby spinach, chopped
- 1/2 cup feta cheese, crumbled
- Fresh parsley or basil, chopped, for garnish (optional)

Instructions:

1. **Preheat the Oven:**
   - Preheat your oven to 180°C (350°F).
2. **Prepare the Eggs:**
   - In a bowl, whisk together eggs, milk or cream, salt, and black pepper until well combined. Set aside.
3. **Sauté the Ingredients:**
   - Heat olive oil in a large oven-safe skillet over medium heat.
   - Add chopped onion and sauté until translucent, about 3-4 minutes.
   - Add minced garlic and cook for another 1 minute until fragrant.
   - Stir in chopped sun-dried tomatoes (bush tomatoes) and baby spinach. Cook for 2-3 minutes until spinach is wilted.
4. **Assemble the Frittata:**
   - Pour the egg mixture evenly over the sautéed vegetables in the skillet.
   - Sprinkle crumbled feta cheese evenly over the top.
5. **Cook the Frittata:**
   - Cook on the stovetop for 3-4 minutes, gently lifting the edges with a spatula to let the uncooked eggs flow underneath.
6. **Bake the Frittata:**
   - Transfer the skillet to the preheated oven.
   - Bake for 12-15 minutes or until the frittata is set in the center and the edges are golden brown.
7. **Serve:**

- Remove the Bush Tomato Frittata from the oven and let it cool slightly.
- Garnish with fresh parsley or basil, if desired.
- Slice into wedges and serve warm or at room temperature.

Tips:

- **Bush Tomatoes:** If you can't find bush tomatoes, you can use regular sun-dried tomatoes. The bush tomatoes impart a unique flavor that adds to the distinctiveness of the frittata.
- **Variations:** Customize your frittata by adding other ingredients such as bell peppers, mushrooms, or cooked bacon.
- **Make-Ahead:** This frittata can be made ahead of time and refrigerated. Reheat gently in the oven or microwave before serving.

Bush Tomato Frittata is a flavorful and versatile dish that can be served for breakfast, brunch, or even a light dinner. Enjoy the robust flavors of bush tomatoes combined with the creamy texture of eggs and feta cheese in every bite!

Macadamia Nut Granola

Ingredients:

- 3 cups rolled oats (old-fashioned oats)
- 1 cup chopped macadamia nuts
- 1/2 cup shredded coconut (unsweetened)
- 1/4 cup honey or maple syrup
- 1/4 cup coconut oil, melted
- 1 teaspoon vanilla extract
- 1/2 teaspoon ground cinnamon
- 1/4 teaspoon salt
- 1/2 cup dried fruits (optional, such as cranberries, apricots, or raisins)

Instructions:

1. **Preheat the Oven:**
   - Preheat your oven to 160°C (325°F). Line a large baking sheet with parchment paper or a silicone baking mat.
2. **Mix Dry Ingredients:**
   - In a large bowl, combine rolled oats, chopped macadamia nuts, shredded coconut, ground cinnamon, and salt. Stir well to mix.
3. **Add Wet Ingredients:**
   - In a separate bowl, whisk together honey or maple syrup, melted coconut oil, and vanilla extract until smooth and well combined.
4. **Combine and Spread:**
   - Pour the wet ingredients over the dry ingredients in the large bowl. Stir until the oats and nuts are evenly coated with the honey/coconut oil mixture.
5. **Bake the Granola:**
   - Spread the granola mixture evenly onto the prepared baking sheet.
   - Bake for 25-30 minutes, stirring halfway through, or until the granola is golden brown and crisp.
6. **Add Dried Fruits (Optional):**
   - If using dried fruits, stir them into the granola immediately after removing from the oven.
7. **Cool and Store:**
   - Allow the Macadamia Nut Granola to cool completely on the baking sheet. As it cools, it will crisp up even more.
   - Once cooled, transfer the granola to an airtight container or jar for storage.

Tips:

- **Customization:** Feel free to customize the granola by adding other nuts, seeds (like chia or flax seeds), or spices (such as nutmeg or cardamom).
- **Sweetness:** Adjust the sweetness by varying the amount of honey or maple syrup according to your taste preferences.
- **Storage:** Store Macadamia Nut Granola in an airtight container at room temperature for up to 2 weeks. It can also be frozen for longer storage.

Macadamia Nut Granola is delicious served with yogurt, milk, or eaten on its own as a crunchy snack. Enjoy the rich, buttery flavor of macadamia nuts combined with the wholesome goodness of oats in this homemade granola recipe!

Kangaroo Sausage Roll

Ingredients:

- 500g kangaroo mince (ground kangaroo meat)
- 1 small onion, finely chopped
- 2 garlic cloves, minced
- 1 tablespoon olive oil
- 1 teaspoon dried mixed herbs (such as thyme, oregano, rosemary)
- Salt and pepper, to taste
- 1/4 cup breadcrumbs
- 2 sheets of puff pastry, thawed if frozen
- 1 egg, beaten (for egg wash)
- Sesame seeds or poppy seeds, for sprinkling (optional)

Instructions:

1. **Preheat the Oven:**
   - Preheat your oven to 200°C (400°F). Line a baking sheet with parchment paper.
2. **Prepare the Filling:**
   - In a frying pan, heat olive oil over medium heat. Add chopped onion and minced garlic. Sauté until onion is translucent, about 3-4 minutes.
   - Add kangaroo mince to the pan, breaking it up with a spoon. Cook for 5-6 minutes until browned and cooked through.
   - Stir in dried herbs, salt, and pepper. Remove from heat and let cool slightly.
   - Once cooled, stir in breadcrumbs to bind the mixture together.
3. **Assemble the Sausage Rolls:**
   - Lay out the thawed puff pastry sheets on a lightly floured surface. Cut each sheet in half lengthwise to make 4 long rectangles.
   - Divide the kangaroo mince mixture into 4 equal portions. Shape each portion into a long sausage shape and place it along the center of each pastry rectangle.
4. **Roll and Seal:**
   - Brush one long edge of each pastry rectangle with beaten egg (this will act as glue).
   - Roll the pastry tightly around the kangaroo mince, sealing the edge with the egg-washed side. Place the rolls seam-side down on the prepared baking sheet.
5. **Bake the Sausage Rolls:**

- Brush the tops of the sausage rolls with beaten egg to give them a golden shine when baked.
- Optional: Sprinkle sesame seeds or poppy seeds on top for extra texture and flavor.
- Bake in the preheated oven for 20-25 minutes, or until the pastry is golden brown and crispy.

6. **Serve:**
   - Remove Kangaroo Sausage Rolls from the oven and let cool slightly before serving.
   - Serve warm with your favorite dipping sauce or enjoy them on their own as a savory snack.

Tips:

- **Variation:** Add grated cheese, diced vegetables (like carrots or bell peppers), or additional herbs to the kangaroo mince mixture for added flavor and texture.
- **Make-Ahead:** You can assemble the sausage rolls ahead of time and refrigerate them until ready to bake. Alternatively, freeze unbaked sausage rolls for up to 1 month. Bake from frozen, adding a few extra minutes to the baking time.
- **Serving Suggestions:** Kangaroo Sausage Rolls are great for picnics, parties, or as a delicious lunch or snack. Pair them with a fresh salad or coleslaw for a complete meal.

Kangaroo Sausage Rolls offer a unique twist on a classic favorite, showcasing the lean and flavorful kangaroo meat wrapped in flaky puff pastry. Enjoy the taste of Australia with this homemade recipe!

Flat White Crepes

Crepe Batter Ingredients:

- 1 cup all-purpose flour
- 2 large eggs
- 1 cup milk
- 1/4 cup water
- 2 tablespoons unsalted butter, melted
- 1 tablespoon sugar (optional, adjust to taste)
- 1 teaspoon vanilla extract
- Pinch of salt

Filling Ingredients:

- 1/2 cup espresso or strong coffee, cooled
- 1/2 cup milk
- 2 tablespoons condensed milk (adjust to taste)
- Whipped cream, for topping
- Cocoa powder or chocolate shavings, for garnish (optional)

Instructions:

1. **Prepare the Crepe Batter:**
    - In a large mixing bowl, whisk together flour, eggs, milk, water, melted butter, sugar (if using), vanilla extract, and a pinch of salt until smooth and well combined. The batter should be thin and pourable. Let the batter rest for at least 15-30 minutes at room temperature.
2. **Cook the Crepes:**
    - Heat a non-stick crepe pan or skillet over medium heat. Lightly grease the pan with butter or cooking spray.
    - Pour a small ladleful of batter into the hot pan, swirling the pan quickly to spread the batter evenly in a thin layer.
    - Cook the crepe for about 1-2 minutes on the first side, or until the edges start to lift and the bottom is lightly golden. Flip the crepe and cook for another 1 minute on the second side. Remove the cooked crepe to a plate and cover to keep warm. Repeat with the remaining batter, stacking the cooked crepes on top of each other.
3. **Prepare the Flat White Filling:**
    - In a small saucepan, heat espresso or strong coffee over medium heat until hot (do not boil).

- Add milk and condensed milk to the coffee, stirring until well combined and heated through. Adjust sweetness with more condensed milk if desired.

4. **Assemble the Flat White Crepes:**
    - Place a crepe on a serving plate. Spoon some of the flat white filling over the crepe, spreading it evenly.
    - Fold the crepe in half, and then in half again to form a triangle shape.
    - Repeat with the remaining crepes and filling.
5. **Serve:**
    - Top each Flat White Crepe with a dollop of whipped cream.
    - Dust with cocoa powder or chocolate shavings for garnish, if desired.
    - Serve immediately while warm.

Tips:

- **Crepe Making Tip:** Adjust the heat as needed to ensure the crepes cook evenly without burning. The first crepe is often a trial to adjust temperature and batter thickness.
- **Variations:** For an extra indulgence, add a drizzle of chocolate sauce or caramel sauce over the crepes before serving.
- **Presentation:** Stack the filled crepes on a platter and serve family-style, or plate individually for a more elegant presentation.

Flat White Crepes combine the delicate texture of crepes with the rich flavors of a flat white coffee, making them a perfect choice for a special breakfast or brunch treat. Enjoy the fusion of French and Australian flavors in this delightful dish!

Golden Gaytime Waffles

Ingredients:

- 1 1/2 cups all-purpose flour
- 2 tablespoons granulated sugar
- 1 tablespoon baking powder
- 1/2 teaspoon salt
- 1 1/4 cups milk
- 1/2 cup unsalted butter, melted
- 2 large eggs
- 1 teaspoon vanilla extract
- 1/2 cup crushed vanilla wafer biscuits (or digestive biscuits)
- Vanilla ice cream, for serving
- Honey or golden syrup, for drizzling
- Crushed nuts (such as almonds or peanuts), for garnish
- Chocolate sauce, for drizzling (optional)

Instructions:

1. **Preheat the Waffle Iron:**
    - Preheat your waffle iron according to manufacturer's instructions.
2. **Prepare the Waffle Batter:**
    - In a large bowl, whisk together flour, sugar, baking powder, and salt.
    - In another bowl, whisk together milk, melted butter, eggs, and vanilla extract until well combined.
    - Pour the wet ingredients into the dry ingredients and stir until just combined. Be careful not to overmix; a few lumps are okay.
    - Gently fold in the crushed vanilla wafer biscuits.
3. **Cook the Waffles:**
    - Lightly grease the preheated waffle iron with non-stick cooking spray or brush with melted butter.
    - Pour enough batter onto the hot waffle iron to cover the grids (amount will depend on the size of your waffle iron). Close the lid and cook according to your waffle iron's instructions until golden brown and crisp.
4. **Assemble the Golden Gaytime Waffles:**
    - Place a cooked waffle on a serving plate.
    - Top with a scoop of vanilla ice cream.
    - Drizzle honey or golden syrup over the ice cream.
    - Sprinkle crushed nuts over the top.

    - Optionally, drizzle with chocolate sauce for extra indulgence.
5. **Serve:**
    - Serve Golden Gaytime Waffles immediately while warm, allowing the ice cream to slightly melt into the waffle.

Tips:

- **Variations:** Instead of vanilla ice cream, you can use caramel or honeycomb-flavored ice cream to mimic the flavors of a Golden Gaytime.
- **Decoration:** Garnish with additional crushed vanilla wafer biscuits or honeycomb candy for extra texture and flavor.
- **Make-Ahead:** Prepare the waffle batter ahead of time and store it in the refrigerator. Cook waffles fresh as needed.

Golden Gaytime Waffles are a delightful combination of crisp waffles, creamy ice cream, crunchy biscuits, and sweet toppings, making them a perfect dessert or indulgent breakfast treat. Enjoy the nostalgic flavors of this Australian favorite in waffle form!

Beetroot and Goat Cheese Salad

Ingredients:

- 3-4 medium-sized beetroots, peeled and cut into wedges
- 2 tablespoons olive oil
- Salt and pepper, to taste
- 4 cups mixed salad greens (such as arugula, spinach, or mesclun)
- 100g goat cheese, crumbled
- 1/4 cup walnuts or pecans, toasted and roughly chopped
- 2 tablespoons balsamic vinegar
- 1 tablespoon honey or maple syrup
- 1/4 cup extra virgin olive oil
- Salt and pepper, to taste

Instructions:

1. **Roast the Beetroots:**
    - Preheat your oven to 200°C (400°F).
    - Place the beetroot wedges on a baking sheet. Drizzle with 2 tablespoons of olive oil and season with salt and pepper. Toss to coat evenly.
    - Roast in the preheated oven for 25-30 minutes, or until the beetroots are tender and caramelized. Remove from the oven and let cool slightly.
2. **Prepare the Salad Dressing:**
    - In a small bowl, whisk together balsamic vinegar, honey or maple syrup, and extra virgin olive oil until well combined. Season with salt and pepper to taste.
3. **Assemble the Salad:**
    - In a large bowl, combine the mixed salad greens with half of the prepared salad dressing. Toss gently to coat the greens.
    - Arrange the dressed greens on a serving platter or individual plates.
    - Top with roasted beetroot wedges.
    - Scatter crumbled goat cheese and toasted walnuts or pecans over the salad.
4. **Serve:**
    - Drizzle the remaining salad dressing over the beetroot and goat cheese salad just before serving.
    - Serve immediately as a side dish or light lunch.

Tips:

- **Variations:** Add sliced fresh strawberries or oranges for a fruity twist. You can also sprinkle with fresh herbs like parsley or dill for added freshness.
- **Make-Ahead:** Roast the beetroots ahead of time and store them in the refrigerator until ready to assemble the salad. Prepare the dressing separately and toss with the salad just before serving to keep the greens fresh.
- **Presentation:** Arrange the salad ingredients neatly on the plate for an elegant presentation. Garnish with extra crumbled goat cheese or a drizzle of balsamic glaze for a finishing touch.

Beetroot and Goat Cheese Salad is not only visually appealing but also packs a flavorful punch with the combination of sweet roasted beets, creamy goat cheese, crunchy nuts, and tangy vinaigrette. Enjoy this salad as a refreshing and nutritious addition to any meal!

Blueberry Damper

Ingredients:

- 2 cups self-raising flour
- 1/4 teaspoon salt
- 1 tablespoon sugar (optional, for sweetness)
- 1/2 cup dried blueberries (or fresh blueberries, if preferred)
- 1/2 cup milk (plus extra if needed)
- 1/4 cup unsalted butter, melted
- Additional butter, for serving

Instructions:

1. **Preheat the Oven:**
   - Preheat your oven to 200°C (400°F). Line a baking sheet with parchment paper.
2. **Prepare the Dough:**
   - In a large mixing bowl, combine self-raising flour, salt, and sugar (if using).
   - Add dried blueberries to the flour mixture and toss to coat them evenly.
3. **Form the Dough:**
   - Make a well in the center of the flour mixture and pour in the milk and melted butter.
   - Using a wooden spoon or your hands, mix until a soft dough forms. Add a little extra milk if the dough is too dry.
4. **Shape the Damper:**
   - Turn the dough out onto a lightly floured surface. Knead gently for a minute until smooth.
   - Shape the dough into a round or oval loaf, about 1 inch (2.5 cm) thick.
5. **Bake the Damper:**
   - Place the shaped damper onto the prepared baking sheet.
   - Using a sharp knife, score the top of the damper with a cross or pattern (this helps it bake evenly).
   - Bake in the preheated oven for 20-25 minutes, or until the damper is golden brown and sounds hollow when tapped on the bottom.
6. **Serve:**
   - Remove the blueberry damper from the oven and let it cool slightly on a wire rack.
   - Serve warm with butter.

Tips:

- **Variations:** Instead of blueberries, you can use other dried fruits like raisins or cranberries, or even add a sprinkle of cinnamon or nutmeg for extra flavor.
- **Outdoor Cooking:** Traditionally, damper is cooked over a campfire. Wrap the dough in foil and cook it in the coals of a campfire for a rustic outdoor experience.
- **Storage:** Store leftover blueberry damper in an airtight container at room temperature for up to 2 days. Warm it slightly before serving.

Blueberry damper is a simple and versatile bread that can be enjoyed as a snack, breakfast, or accompaniment to meals. Its soft texture and bursts of blueberries make it a delightful treat, whether enjoyed fresh out of the oven or on a picnic.

Spinach and Cheese Pie

Ingredients:

- 1 tablespoon olive oil
- 1 onion, finely chopped
- 2 garlic cloves, minced
- 500g fresh spinach leaves, washed and roughly chopped
- Salt and pepper, to taste
- 200g feta cheese, crumbled
- 100g ricotta cheese
- 1/2 cup grated Parmesan cheese
- 3 large eggs, lightly beaten
- 1/4 teaspoon ground nutmeg (optional)
- 1 sheet puff pastry, thawed if frozen
- 1 egg, beaten (for egg wash)

Instructions:

1. **Prepare the Filling:**
    - In a large skillet or frying pan, heat olive oil over medium heat. Add chopped onion and garlic, sauté until softened and fragrant, about 3-4 minutes.
    - Add chopped spinach to the pan in batches, stirring until wilted. Cook for another 3-4 minutes until most of the moisture has evaporated.
    - Season with salt and pepper to taste. Remove from heat and let cool slightly.
2. **Make the Cheese Mixture:**
    - In a large mixing bowl, combine crumbled feta cheese, ricotta cheese, grated Parmesan cheese, beaten eggs, and ground nutmeg (if using). Mix until well combined.
    - Add the cooked spinach mixture to the cheese mixture. Stir until evenly incorporated.
3. **Assemble the Pie:**
    - Preheat your oven to 200°C (400°F). Line a baking sheet with parchment paper.
    - Roll out the thawed puff pastry sheet on a lightly floured surface into a rectangle (approximately 10x14 inches or 25x35 cm).
4. **Fill and Fold the Pie:**

- Spread the spinach and cheese mixture evenly over one half of the puff pastry sheet, leaving a border around the edges.
- Fold the other half of the pastry over the filling to cover, pressing the edges together to seal. Crimp the edges with a fork or twist them to seal tightly.

5. **Bake the Pie:**
    - Transfer the assembled pie onto the prepared baking sheet.
    - Brush the top of the pie with beaten egg to give it a golden color when baked.
    - Using a sharp knife, make a few small slits in the top of the pie to allow steam to escape.
    - Bake in the preheated oven for 25-30 minutes, or until the pastry is golden brown and crisp.
6. **Serve:**
    - Remove the Spinach and Cheese Pie from the oven and let it cool slightly before slicing.
    - Serve warm or at room temperature as a delicious main dish or side.

Tips:

- **Variations:** Add chopped cooked bacon or mushrooms to the spinach mixture for added flavor and texture.
- **Make-Ahead:** You can prepare the spinach and cheese filling ahead of time and assemble the pie just before baking. Alternatively, bake the pie ahead and reheat gently in the oven before serving.
- **Storage:** Leftover Spinach and Cheese Pie can be stored in an airtight container in the refrigerator for up to 3 days. Reheat in the oven until warmed through before serving.

Spinach and Cheese Pie is a comforting and satisfying dish that combines the goodness of spinach with creamy cheeses, all encased in buttery puff pastry. Enjoy this savory pie for a hearty meal with family and friends!

Pumpkin Scone with Jam

Ingredients:

- 2 cups self-raising flour
- 1/4 cup caster sugar
- 1/2 teaspoon ground cinnamon
- 1/4 teaspoon ground nutmeg
- Pinch of salt
- 60g unsalted butter, chilled and cubed
- 1/2 cup mashed pumpkin (cooked and cooled)
- 1/4 cup milk (plus extra if needed)
- 1 teaspoon vanilla extract
- Jam of your choice, for serving

Instructions:

1. **Preheat the Oven:**
    - Preheat your oven to 200°C (400°F). Line a baking sheet with parchment paper.
2. **Prepare the Dough:**
    - In a large mixing bowl, sift together self-raising flour, caster sugar, ground cinnamon, ground nutmeg, and a pinch of salt.
    - Add chilled butter cubes to the flour mixture. Use your fingertips to rub the butter into the flour until it resembles breadcrumbs.
3. **Mix the Wet Ingredients:**
    - In a separate bowl, combine mashed pumpkin, milk, and vanilla extract. Stir until smooth.
4. **Combine and Knead:**
    - Make a well in the center of the dry ingredients. Pour the pumpkin mixture into the well.
    - Use a butter knife or spatula to mix until the dough starts to come together. If the dough is too dry, add a little more milk, 1 tablespoon at a time, until the dough forms a soft ball.
5. **Shape the Scones:**
    - Turn the dough out onto a lightly floured surface. Pat the dough into a round shape about 2.5 cm (1 inch) thick.
    - Use a floured round cutter (about 5 cm or 2 inches in diameter) to cut out scones. Place the scones on the prepared baking sheet, leaving a little space between them.

6. **Bake the Scones:**
   - Bake in the preheated oven for 12-15 minutes, or until the scones are risen and golden brown on top.
   - Remove from the oven and transfer the scones to a wire rack to cool slightly.
7. **Serve:**
   - Split the warm scones in half and spread with your favorite jam (such as strawberry, raspberry, or apricot).
   - Serve Pumpkin Scones with Jam warm or at room temperature.

Tips:

- **Variations:** Add a handful of raisins or chopped nuts to the dough for extra texture and flavor.
- **Storage:** Store leftover scones in an airtight container at room temperature for up to 2 days. Warm them in the oven or microwave before serving.
- **Presentation:** Dust the tops of the scones with a little powdered sugar for an extra touch of sweetness before serving.

Pumpkin Scones with Jam are a delicious twist on the classic scone, perfect for morning or afternoon tea. Enjoy the warm, comforting flavors of pumpkin and jam in every bite!

Tim Tam Banana Bread

Ingredients:

- 1 3/4 cups all-purpose flour
- 1 teaspoon baking powder
- 1/2 teaspoon baking soda
- 1/2 teaspoon salt
- 1/2 cup unsalted butter, softened
- 1/2 cup granulated sugar
- 1/2 cup brown sugar, packed
- 2 large eggs
- 1 teaspoon vanilla extract
- 3 ripe bananas, mashed
- 1/2 cup Greek yogurt (or sour cream)
- 1 cup crushed Tim Tam biscuits (about 8-10 biscuits)
- Additional Tim Tam biscuits, halved lengthwise (for topping, optional)

Instructions:

1. **Preheat the Oven:**
   - Preheat your oven to 180°C (350°F). Grease and line a 9x5-inch loaf pan with parchment paper, leaving an overhang on the sides for easy removal.
2. **Prepare the Dry Ingredients:**
   - In a medium bowl, whisk together flour, baking powder, baking soda, and salt. Set aside.
3. **Cream Butter and Sugars:**
   - In a large bowl or the bowl of a stand mixer, cream together softened butter, granulated sugar, and brown sugar until light and fluffy, about 2-3 minutes.
4. **Add Eggs and Vanilla:**
   - Add eggs, one at a time, mixing well after each addition. Add vanilla extract and mix until combined.
5. **Combine Wet and Dry Ingredients:**
   - Add mashed bananas and Greek yogurt (or sour cream) to the butter mixture. Mix until well combined.
   - Gradually add the dry ingredients to the wet ingredients, mixing until just combined. Do not overmix.
6. **Fold in Tim Tam Biscuits:**

- Gently fold in the crushed Tim Tam biscuits until evenly distributed throughout the batter.

7. **Bake the Banana Bread:**
   - Pour the batter into the prepared loaf pan, spreading it evenly. If desired, arrange halved Tim Tam biscuits on top of the batter for decoration.
   - Bake in the preheated oven for 55-65 minutes, or until a toothpick inserted into the center comes out clean or with a few moist crumbs.

8. **Cool and Serve:**
   - Allow the Tim Tam Banana Bread to cool in the pan for 10 minutes before transferring to a wire rack to cool completely.
   - Slice and serve warm or at room temperature.

Tips:

- **Tim Tam Variation:** You can use any flavor of Tim Tam biscuits for this recipe, such as original, dark chocolate, or caramel.
- **Storage:** Store leftover Tim Tam Banana Bread in an airtight container at room temperature for up to 3 days, or refrigerate for longer freshness.
- **Serve with:** Enjoy slices of Tim Tam Banana Bread on its own, or with a dollop of whipped cream, ice cream, or a drizzle of caramel sauce for extra indulgence.

Tim Tam Banana Bread is a delightful way to enjoy the iconic Australian biscuit flavor in a moist and flavorful banana bread. Perfect for breakfast, brunch, or as a sweet treat with tea or coffee!

Fairy Bread Pancakes

Ingredients:

- 1 cup all-purpose flour
- 2 tablespoons granulated sugar
- 1 teaspoon baking powder
- 1/2 teaspoon baking soda
- Pinch of salt
- 1 cup buttermilk (or 1 cup milk mixed with 1 tablespoon vinegar or lemon juice)
- 1 large egg
- 2 tablespoons unsalted butter, melted
- 1 teaspoon vanilla extract
- Butter or oil, for cooking
- Sprinkles (hundreds and thousands), for topping
- Whipped cream, for serving (optional)
- Maple syrup, for serving

Instructions:

1. **Prepare the Pancake Batter:**
   - In a large bowl, whisk together the flour, sugar, baking powder, baking soda, and salt.
   - In another bowl, whisk together the buttermilk, egg, melted butter, and vanilla extract until well combined.
   - Pour the wet ingredients into the dry ingredients and stir until just combined. The batter should be slightly lumpy.
2. **Cook the Pancakes:**
   - Heat a non-stick skillet or griddle over medium heat. Lightly grease with butter or oil.
   - Pour 1/4 cup of batter onto the skillet for each pancake. Cook until bubbles form on the surface of the pancake and the edges begin to look set, about 2-3 minutes.
   - Flip the pancake and cook until the other side is golden brown, about 1-2 minutes more. Repeat with the remaining batter.
3. **Assemble Fairy Bread Pancakes:**
   - Stack the pancakes on serving plates.
   - Sprinkle a generous amount of hundreds and thousands (sprinkles) over the top of each pancake stack while they are still warm, pressing gently so the sprinkles stick.

4. **Serve:**
    - Optionally, top with a dollop of whipped cream and drizzle with maple syrup.
    - Serve Fairy Bread Pancakes warm and enjoy the colorful, festive treat!

Tips:

- **Variations:** Experiment with different types of sprinkles for varied colors and flavors. You can also add a dash of almond extract to the batter for a subtle nutty flavor.
- **Presentation:** Arrange the pancakes on a platter or individual plates, garnished with extra sprinkles for a fun and festive look.
- **Make-Ahead:** You can prepare the pancake batter ahead of time and refrigerate it overnight. Stir the batter well before cooking.

Fairy Bread Pancakes are a delightful treat that brings the joy and whimsy of fairy bread to a breakfast classic. Enjoy these colorful pancakes for a special occasion or anytime you want to add a touch of fun to your morning meal!

Crocodile Crepes

Ingredients:

For the Crepes:

- 1 cup all-purpose flour
- 2 large eggs
- 1 cup milk
- 1/4 cup water
- 2 tablespoons unsalted butter, melted
- 1 tablespoon granulated sugar
- 1/4 teaspoon salt
- Butter or oil, for cooking

For the Filling:

- 200g crocodile meat, thinly sliced (substitute with chicken or shrimp if crocodile meat is not available)
- 1 tablespoon olive oil
- 1 garlic clove, minced
- 1/2 onion, finely chopped
- 1 bell pepper (red or green), diced
- 1 cup mushrooms, sliced
- Salt and pepper, to taste
- 1/2 cup heavy cream
- 1/2 cup shredded cheese (such as mozzarella or cheddar)
- Fresh herbs (such as parsley or chives), chopped (for garnish)

Instructions:

1. **Prepare the Crepe Batter:**
    - In a large mixing bowl, whisk together flour, eggs, milk, water, melted butter, sugar, and salt until smooth. Let the batter rest for at least 30 minutes.
2. **Cook the Crepes:**
    - Heat a non-stick skillet or crepe pan over medium heat. Lightly grease the pan with butter or oil.
    - Pour about 1/4 cup of batter into the pan, swirling it around to coat the bottom evenly.

- Cook the crepe for about 1-2 minutes, until the edges start to lift and the bottom is golden brown. Flip the crepe and cook for another 1-2 minutes on the other side. Repeat with the remaining batter, stacking the cooked crepes on a plate.
3. **Prepare the Filling:**
    - In a large skillet or frying pan, heat olive oil over medium heat. Add minced garlic and chopped onion, sauté until softened and fragrant.
    - Add thinly sliced crocodile meat (or substitute), diced bell pepper, and sliced mushrooms to the pan. Cook until the crocodile meat is cooked through and vegetables are tender, about 5-7 minutes.
    - Season with salt and pepper to taste.
    - Pour in heavy cream and bring to a simmer. Cook for another 2-3 minutes until the sauce thickens slightly.
    - Stir in shredded cheese until melted and well combined. Remove from heat.
4. **Assemble the Crocodile Crepes:**
    - Spoon a portion of the filling onto each crepe, spreading it evenly over one half of the crepe.
    - Fold the crepe in half over the filling, then fold in half again to form a triangle shape.
5. **Serve:**
    - Arrange the filled crepes on serving plates.
    - Garnish with chopped fresh herbs, such as parsley or chives.
    - Serve Crocodile Crepes warm, as a main dish or hearty appetizer.

Tips:

- **Variations:** You can customize the filling with your favorite ingredients, such as spinach, sun-dried tomatoes, or different types of cheese.
- **Make-Ahead:** Prepare the crepes and filling separately ahead of time. Store the crepes stacked with parchment paper in between to prevent sticking. Reheat the filling gently before assembling.
- **Presentation:** Arrange the filled crepes on a platter and garnish with additional herbs for a colorful and appetizing presentation.

Crocodile Crepes offer a unique culinary experience, combining tender meat with savory vegetables and creamy sauce wrapped in delicate crepes. Enjoy this Australian-inspired dish for a flavorful meal that's sure to impress!

Emu Poached Eggs

Ingredients:

- Emu eggs (1 per serving)
- Water
- Vinegar (optional)
- Salt and pepper, to taste

Instructions:

1. **Prepare the Emu Eggs:**
   - Emu eggs are significantly larger than chicken eggs, so one emu egg can be equivalent to about 10-12 chicken eggs in volume.
   - Carefully crack the emu egg and separate the egg white and yolk into different bowls.
2. **Poaching the Emu Eggs:**
   - Fill a large saucepan with water, making sure there's enough water to cover the eggs once they're submerged.
   - Bring the water to a gentle simmer over medium heat. If desired, add a splash of vinegar to the water (this helps the egg whites to coagulate quicker).
   - Gently slide the emu egg into the simmering water, taking care not to break the yolk.
   - Poach the egg for about 8-10 minutes, or until the egg white is cooked through and the yolk is still runny.
3. **Remove and Serve:**
   - Carefully remove the poached emu egg using a slotted spoon, allowing excess water to drain.
   - Season with salt and pepper to taste, and serve immediately while still warm.

Tips:

- **Handling Emu Eggs:** Emu eggs have a thicker shell compared to chicken eggs, so cracking them may require a bit more force.
- **Cooking Time:** Cooking time can vary depending on the size of the emu egg and desired level of doneness. Adjust cooking time accordingly.
- **Presentation:** Serve emu poached eggs on toast, English muffins, or with a side of greens for a delicious and unique breakfast or brunch option.

Emu poached eggs offer a rich and flavorful twist on traditional poached eggs, making them a memorable addition to any breakfast or brunch menu. Enjoy the unique taste and texture of emu eggs with this simple cooking method!

Sausage Roll Pancakes

Ingredients:

- 6 sausages (pork, beef, or chicken)
- 1 cup all-purpose flour
- 1 tablespoon baking powder
- 1/2 teaspoon salt
- 1 tablespoon granulated sugar
- 1 cup milk
- 1 large egg
- 2 tablespoons unsalted butter, melted
- Butter or oil, for cooking
- Maple syrup, for serving

Instructions:

1. **Cook the Sausages:**
    - Preheat your oven to 200°C (400°F). Line a baking sheet with parchment paper.
    - Place sausages on the baking sheet and bake for 20-25 minutes, or until cooked through. Remove from the oven and let them cool slightly. Once cooled, slice each sausage into smaller pieces, about 2-3 inches long.
2. **Prepare the Pancake Batter:**
    - In a large bowl, whisk together the flour, baking powder, salt, and sugar.
    - In another bowl, whisk together the milk, egg, and melted butter until well combined.
    - Pour the wet ingredients into the dry ingredients and stir until just combined. The batter should be slightly lumpy.
3. **Cook the Pancakes:**
    - Heat a non-stick skillet or griddle over medium heat. Lightly grease the surface with butter or oil.
    - Pour about 1/4 cup of batter onto the skillet for each pancake. Immediately place a piece of sausage on top of each pancake.
    - Cook until bubbles form on the surface of the pancake and the edges begin to look set, about 2-3 minutes.
    - Flip the pancake and cook for another 1-2 minutes, until the other side is golden brown and the sausage is heated through.
4. **Serve:**

- Remove the sausage roll pancakes from the skillet and place them on a serving plate.
- Serve warm with maple syrup drizzled over the top.

Tips:

- **Variations:** Experiment with different types of sausages, such as spicy chorizo or chicken apple sausage, for varied flavors.
- **Make-Ahead:** You can prepare the sausage pieces and pancake batter ahead of time. Store the sausage in the refrigerator and the batter in an airtight container in the refrigerator for up to 24 hours. Stir the batter well before cooking.
- **Presentation:** Arrange the sausage roll pancakes on a platter and serve them family-style for a hearty breakfast or brunch.

Sausage Roll Pancakes combine the savory goodness of sausage rolls with the comforting appeal of fluffy pancakes, making them a delicious and satisfying meal option. Enjoy this unique twist on traditional pancakes for a delightful breakfast or brunch treat!

Damper with Jam and Cream

Ingredients:

- 3 cups self-raising flour
- Pinch of salt
- 1 cup milk
- 1/2 cup water
- Jam (such as strawberry or raspberry), for serving
- Whipped cream, for serving

Instructions:

1. **Preheat the Oven:**
    - Preheat your oven to 200°C (400°F). Line a baking sheet with parchment paper.
2. **Prepare the Damper Dough:**
    - In a large bowl, sift the self-raising flour and salt together.
    - Make a well in the center of the flour mixture and pour in the milk and water.
    - Use a butter knife or spatula to mix until a soft dough forms. The dough should come together but not be too sticky.
3. **Shape and Bake the Damper:**
    - Turn the dough out onto a lightly floured surface. Shape it into a round loaf, about 1.5-2 inches thick.
    - Place the damper onto the prepared baking sheet. Use a sharp knife to score a cross pattern on the top of the loaf, about halfway through the dough.
    - Bake in the preheated oven for 30-35 minutes, or until the damper is golden brown and sounds hollow when tapped on the bottom.
4. **Serve:**
    - Remove the damper from the oven and let it cool slightly on a wire rack.
    - Once cooled, slice the damper into wedges or thick slices.
    - Serve the damper with jam and whipped cream on the side.

Tips:

- **Variations:** Add a tablespoon of sugar to the flour mixture if you prefer a slightly sweeter damper.

- **Toppings:** Aside from jam and cream, you can also enjoy damper with butter, honey, or even savory toppings like cheese and tomato.
- **Storage:** Damper is best enjoyed fresh on the day it's baked. Store any leftovers in an airtight container at room temperature and toast slices before serving.

Damper with jam and cream is a deliciously rustic and comforting treat, perfect for breakfast, brunch, or a simple afternoon tea. Enjoy the soft, fluffy texture of the damper with the sweetness of jam and richness of whipped cream for a delightful Australian culinary experience!

Anzac Biscuit Muffins

Ingredients:

- 1 cup rolled oats
- 1 cup all-purpose flour
- 1/2 cup brown sugar
- 1/4 cup desiccated coconut
- 1/2 teaspoon baking soda
- 1/4 cup golden syrup or honey
- 1/2 cup unsalted butter, melted
- 1/4 cup boiling water
- 1 teaspoon vanilla extract
- 1/2 cup chopped dried apricots (optional)

Instructions:

1. **Preheat the Oven:**
   - Preheat your oven to 180°C (350°F). Line a muffin tin with paper liners or grease the muffin cups.
2. **Prepare the Dry Ingredients:**
   - In a large bowl, combine rolled oats, all-purpose flour, brown sugar, desiccated coconut, and baking soda. Stir to combine.
3. **Combine Wet Ingredients:**
   - In a separate bowl, whisk together golden syrup (or honey), melted butter, boiling water, and vanilla extract until smooth.
4. **Mix the Batter:**
   - Pour the wet ingredients into the dry ingredients. Stir until just combined. If using, fold in chopped dried apricots.
5. **Fill the Muffin Cups:**
   - Spoon the batter evenly into the prepared muffin cups, filling each about 2/3 full.
6. **Bake the Muffins:**
   - Bake in the preheated oven for 15-18 minutes, or until the muffins are golden brown and a toothpick inserted into the center comes out clean.
7. **Cool and Serve:**
   - Remove the muffins from the tin and transfer them to a wire rack to cool completely.
   - Serve Anzac Biscuit Muffins warm or at room temperature.

Tips:

- **Variations:** Add chopped nuts, raisins, or chocolate chips to the batter for extra flavor and texture.
- **Storage:** Store leftover muffins in an airtight container at room temperature for up to 3 days. They can also be frozen for longer storage.
- **Serve with:** Enjoy Anzac Biscuit Muffins on their own, or with a dollop of yogurt or a drizzle of honey for added sweetness.

Anzac Biscuit Muffins offer a delightful twist on the classic Anzac biscuits, combining the beloved flavors of oats, coconut, and golden syrup in a convenient muffin form. Perfect for breakfast, brunch, or as a snack with tea or coffee!

Kangaroo Stuffed Mushrooms

Ingredients:

- 12 large mushrooms (portobello or similar)
- 250g ground kangaroo meat
- 1/2 onion, finely chopped
- 2 cloves garlic, minced
- 1/2 cup breadcrumbs
- 1/4 cup grated Parmesan cheese
- 1 tablespoon olive oil
- Salt and pepper, to taste
- Fresh parsley or thyme, chopped (for garnish)

Instructions:

1. **Prepare the Mushrooms:**
   - Preheat your oven to 180°C (350°F). Line a baking sheet with parchment paper.
   - Clean the mushrooms with a damp cloth or paper towel to remove any dirt. Remove the stems and finely chop them for later use.
2. **Prepare the Filling:**
   - In a skillet, heat olive oil over medium heat. Add chopped onion and minced garlic. Sauté until onions are translucent and garlic is fragrant.
   - Add ground kangaroo meat and chopped mushroom stems to the skillet. Cook until the kangaroo meat is browned and cooked through, breaking it up with a spoon as it cooks.
   - Stir in breadcrumbs and cook for another minute, allowing them to absorb any excess moisture.
   - Remove from heat and stir in grated Parmesan cheese. Season with salt and pepper to taste.
3. **Stuff the Mushrooms:**
   - Spoon the kangaroo meat mixture into each mushroom cap, filling them evenly.
4. **Bake the Stuffed Mushrooms:**
   - Place the stuffed mushrooms on the prepared baking sheet.
   - Bake in the preheated oven for 15-20 minutes, or until the mushrooms are tender and the filling is heated through.
5. **Serve:**

- Remove the stuffed mushrooms from the oven and garnish with chopped fresh parsley or thyme.
- Serve Kangaroo Stuffed Mushrooms warm as a delicious appetizer or main dish.

Tips:

- **Variations:** You can substitute kangaroo meat with ground beef, turkey, or chicken if kangaroo meat is not available.
- **Cheese:** Feel free to experiment with different types of cheese for added flavor, such as cheddar or mozzarella.
- **Presentation:** Arrange the stuffed mushrooms on a platter and garnish with additional herbs for a beautiful presentation.

Kangaroo Stuffed Mushrooms offer a unique and flavorful dish that's perfect for showcasing the distinctive taste of kangaroo meat. Enjoy these stuffed mushrooms as a delightful appetizer or part of a main meal!

Tim Tam Crepes

Ingredients:

- 1 cup all-purpose flour
- 2 large eggs
- 1 cup milk
- 1/4 cup water
- 2 tablespoons unsalted butter, melted
- 1 tablespoon granulated sugar
- Pinch of salt
- 1 teaspoon vanilla extract
- Tim Tam biscuits (original or preferred flavor), crushed
- Whipped cream, for serving
- Chocolate sauce or caramel sauce, for drizzling

Instructions:

1. **Prepare the Crepe Batter:**
    - In a large mixing bowl, whisk together the flour, sugar, and salt.
    - In another bowl, whisk together the eggs, milk, water, melted butter, and vanilla extract until well combined.
    - Pour the wet ingredients into the dry ingredients and whisk until smooth. The batter should be thin and pourable. If needed, add more milk or water to adjust the consistency.
2. **Cook the Crepes:**
    - Heat a non-stick skillet or crepe pan over medium heat. Lightly grease the pan with butter or oil.
    - Pour about 1/4 cup of batter into the skillet, swirling it around to coat the bottom evenly. Cook for about 1-2 minutes, or until the edges start to lift and the bottom is golden brown.
    - Flip the crepe and cook for another 1-2 minutes on the other side. Repeat with the remaining batter, stacking the cooked crepes on a plate.
3. **Assemble the Tim Tam Crepes:**
    - Spread a layer of crushed Tim Tam biscuits over each crepe while still warm.
    - Roll or fold the crepes into quarters or desired shape.
4. **Serve:**
    - Arrange the Tim Tam crepes on serving plates.

- Top with a dollop of whipped cream and drizzle with chocolate sauce or caramel sauce.
- Serve Tim Tam Crepes warm and enjoy the rich, chocolatey flavors!

Tips:

- **Variations:** Experiment with different flavors of Tim Tam biscuits, such as dark chocolate, caramel, or white chocolate.
- **Presentation:** Garnish with additional crushed Tim Tam biscuits or chocolate shavings for extra texture and visual appeal.
- **Make-Ahead:** You can prepare the crepes ahead of time and store them in the refrigerator, layered between parchment paper. Reheat gently before serving.

Tim Tam Crepes offer a delightful combination of soft, thin crepes filled with the crunchy texture and rich flavor of Tim Tam biscuits, topped with creamy whipped cream and decadent sauce. Enjoy these indulgent crepes as a special dessert or treat!

Vegemite and Cheese Pie

Ingredients:

- 1 sheet of pre-made shortcrust pastry, thawed
- 1 sheet of pre-made puff pastry, thawed
- 2 tablespoons Vegemite (adjust to taste)
- 1 cup grated cheese (cheddar or tasty cheese)
- 1 egg, beaten (for egg wash)

Instructions:

1. **Preheat the Oven:**
   - Preheat your oven to 200°C (400°F).
2. **Prepare the Pie Base:**
   - Roll out the shortcrust pastry sheet on a lightly floured surface to fit into a pie dish. Place the pastry into the pie dish and trim any excess around the edges.
3. **Spread Vegemite:**
   - Spread Vegemite evenly over the base of the pastry. Adjust the amount according to your preference for Vegemite flavor.
4. **Add Cheese:**
   - Sprinkle grated cheese evenly over the Vegemite layer.
5. **Top with Puff Pastry:**
   - Roll out the puff pastry sheet on a lightly floured surface to slightly larger than the pie dish. Place the puff pastry over the cheese layer, pressing the edges to seal with the shortcrust pastry.
6. **Ventilation:**
   - Use a sharp knife to make a few small slits or vents in the top of the pie to allow steam to escape during baking.
7. **Egg Wash:**
   - Brush the top of the pie with beaten egg to create a golden crust when baked.
8. **Bake the Pie:**
   - Place the pie dish on a baking tray and bake in the preheated oven for 25-30 minutes, or until the pastry is golden brown and cooked through.
9. **Serve:**
   - Remove from the oven and let the pie cool slightly before slicing and serving.

Tips:

- **Cheese:** Experiment with different types of cheese for varied flavors. Sharp cheddar or tasty cheese works well with Vegemite.
- **Variations:** Add sliced tomatoes or caramelized onions between the Vegemite and cheese layers for extra flavor and texture.
- **Storage:** Store any leftover pie in an airtight container in the refrigerator for up to 3 days. Reheat in the oven or microwave before serving.

Vegemite and Cheese Pie is a savory and comforting dish that celebrates the unique flavors of Australia's iconic spread. Enjoy it warm as a delicious snack or part of a meal!

Lamington Crepes

Ingredients:

For the Crepes:

- 1 cup all-purpose flour
- 2 large eggs
- 1 cup milk
- 1/4 cup water
- 2 tablespoons unsalted butter, melted
- 1 tablespoon granulated sugar
- Pinch of salt

For the Filling:

- 1 cup whipped cream
- 1/2 cup raspberry jam or strawberry jam

For the Coating:

- 2 cups shredded coconut (desiccated coconut)
- 1 cup chocolate ganache (or melted chocolate)

Instructions:

1. **Prepare the Crepes:**
     - In a large mixing bowl, whisk together the flour, sugar, and salt.
     - In another bowl, whisk together the eggs, milk, water, and melted butter until well combined.
     - Pour the wet ingredients into the dry ingredients and whisk until smooth. The batter should be thin and pourable.
2. **Cook the Crepes:**
     - Heat a non-stick skillet or crepe pan over medium heat. Lightly grease the pan with butter or oil.
     - Pour about 1/4 cup of batter into the skillet, swirling it around to coat the bottom evenly. Cook for about 1-2 minutes, or until the edges start to lift and the bottom is golden brown.
     - Flip the crepe and cook for another 1-2 minutes on the other side. Repeat with the remaining batter, stacking the cooked crepes on a plate.
3. **Assemble the Lamington Crepes:**

- Lay a crepe flat on a clean surface.
- Spread a layer of whipped cream over the crepe, leaving a small border around the edges.
- Spoon a layer of raspberry or strawberry jam over the whipped cream.
- Roll up the crepe tightly into a cylinder shape. Repeat with the remaining crepes.

4. **Coat the Crepes:**
    - Spread the shredded coconut on a plate.
    - Dip each rolled crepe into the chocolate ganache or melted chocolate, coating it evenly.
    - Immediately roll the coated crepe in the shredded coconut, pressing gently to adhere the coconut to the chocolate.

5. **Serve:**
    - Transfer the Lamington Crepes to a serving platter or individual plates.
    - Serve immediately, or refrigerate for 15-20 minutes to allow the chocolate to set before serving.

Tips:

- **Ganache:** To make chocolate ganache, heat 1 cup of heavy cream until simmering, then pour over 8 ounces of chopped chocolate. Stir until smooth and glossy.
- **Variations:** You can add a sprinkle of powdered sugar on top or drizzle extra chocolate ganache for added decadence.
- **Presentation:** Arrange the Lamington Crepes on a platter and garnish with fresh berries or mint leaves for a colorful presentation.

Lamington Crepes offer a delightful fusion of flavors and textures, combining the lightness of crepes with the sweetness of jam, creaminess of whipped cream, and the crunch of shredded coconut. Enjoy these as a special dessert or treat for any occasion!

Barbecue Chicken Toast

Ingredients:

- 2 slices of bread (white, whole wheat, or your preferred type)
- 1/2 cup shredded cooked chicken (rotisserie chicken works well)
- 1/4 cup barbecue sauce (your favorite brand or homemade)
- 1/2 cup shredded cheese (cheddar, mozzarella, or a blend)
- Fresh parsley or green onions, chopped (optional, for garnish)

Instructions:

1. **Prepare the Toast:**
    - Preheat your oven's broiler or toaster oven.
    - Place the bread slices on a baking sheet lined with parchment paper or foil.
2. **Prepare the Barbecue Chicken:**
    - In a small bowl, mix the shredded cooked chicken with barbecue sauce until well coated.
3. **Assemble the Toast:**
    - Spread the barbecue chicken evenly over the bread slices.
    - Sprinkle the shredded cheese on top of the barbecue chicken layer.
4. **Broil the Toast:**
    - Place the baking sheet under the broiler or in the toaster oven.
    - Broil for 3-5 minutes, or until the cheese is melted and bubbly, and the edges of the bread are toasted.
5. **Serve:**
    - Remove from the oven and let cool slightly.
    - Garnish with chopped parsley or green onions, if desired.
    - Serve Barbecue Chicken Toast warm as a quick and tasty snack or light meal.

Tips:

- **Variations:** Add sliced onions, bell peppers, or jalapeños for extra flavor and texture.
- **Chicken:** Use leftover grilled or roasted chicken for added flavor.
- **Cheese:** Experiment with different types of cheese or a cheese blend for varied flavors.

- **Presentation:** Serve Barbecue Chicken Toast with a side salad or coleslaw for a complete meal.

Barbecue Chicken Toast is a simple and delicious way to enjoy the flavors of barbecue chicken in a convenient open-faced sandwich format. It's perfect for a quick lunch, snack, or even as an appetizer for gatherings!

Pavlova Toast

Ingredients:

- 2 slices of bread (white, whole wheat, or your preferred type)
- 1/2 cup whipped cream or Greek yogurt
- Fresh fruits (such as strawberries, kiwi, berries, or mango), sliced
- 2 tablespoons fruit jam or fruit compote (optional)
- Honey or maple syrup, for drizzling
- Mint leaves, for garnish (optional)

Instructions:

1. **Prepare the Toast:**
    - Toast the bread slices until golden brown and crispy. You can use a toaster or toast them in a skillet with a bit of butter for extra flavor.
2. **Assemble the Pavlova Toast:**
    - Spread a layer of whipped cream or Greek yogurt evenly over each toasted bread slice.
    - Arrange the sliced fresh fruits on top of the whipped cream or yogurt. Be creative with the arrangement and use a variety of colorful fruits.
    - If desired, spoon a small amount of fruit jam or compote over the fruits for extra sweetness.
3. **Serve:**
    - Drizzle honey or maple syrup over the Pavlova Toast for added sweetness.
    - Garnish with mint leaves for a fresh touch.
    - Serve Pavlova Toast immediately as a delightful breakfast, brunch, or dessert.

Tips:

- **Variations:** Experiment with different combinations of fruits. You can also add shredded coconut, nuts, or chocolate shavings for extra texture.
- **Creamy Topping:** Instead of whipped cream or Greek yogurt, you can use mascarpone cheese or a flavored cream cheese spread.
- **Presentation:** Serve Pavlova Toast on a platter or individual plates for an elegant presentation. It's a perfect treat for special occasions or gatherings.

Pavlova Toast offers a delightful blend of crispy toast, creamy topping, and fresh fruits, reminiscent of the beloved Pavlova dessert. Enjoy this unique and delicious twist on a classic!

Barbecue Bacon Pancakes

Ingredients:

- 6 slices of bacon
- 1 cup all-purpose flour
- 1 tablespoon granulated sugar
- 1 teaspoon baking powder
- 1/2 teaspoon baking soda
- Pinch of salt
- 1 cup buttermilk
- 1 large egg
- 2 tablespoons unsalted butter, melted
- 1/4 cup barbecue sauce (your favorite brand or homemade)
- Maple syrup, for serving

Instructions:

1. **Cook the Bacon:**
    - Heat a large skillet over medium heat. Add the bacon slices and cook until crispy. Transfer the cooked bacon to a plate lined with paper towels to drain excess grease. Once cooled, chop or crumble the bacon into small pieces.
2. **Prepare the Pancake Batter:**
    - In a large bowl, whisk together the flour, sugar, baking powder, baking soda, and salt.
    - In another bowl, whisk together the buttermilk, egg, and melted butter until smooth.
    - Pour the wet ingredients into the dry ingredients and stir until just combined. Be careful not to overmix; a few lumps in the batter are okay.
3. **Cook the Pancakes:**
    - Heat a non-stick skillet or griddle over medium heat. Lightly grease the surface with butter or cooking spray.
    - Pour about 1/4 cup of batter onto the skillet for each pancake. Cook until bubbles form on the surface of the pancake and the edges look set, about 2-3 minutes.
    - Flip the pancakes and cook for another 1-2 minutes, or until golden brown and cooked through.
    - Repeat with the remaining batter, adjusting the heat as needed.
4. **Assemble the Barbecue Bacon Pancakes:**

- Place a pancake on a serving plate. Spread a thin layer of barbecue sauce over the pancake.
- Sprinkle a generous amount of chopped bacon pieces over the barbecue sauce.
- Stack another pancake on top and repeat the layers of barbecue sauce and bacon.
- Continue stacking until you have used all the pancakes, ending with a pancake on top.

5. **Serve:**
   - Drizzle maple syrup over the top of the stack of pancakes.
   - Optionally, garnish with extra bacon pieces or chopped green onions.
   - Serve Barbecue Bacon Pancakes warm as a hearty and savory breakfast or brunch dish.

Tips:

- **Variations:** Add a slice of melted cheese between the layers of pancakes for extra richness and flavor.
- **Make-Ahead:** You can cook the bacon ahead of time and store it in the refrigerator. Reheat before assembling the pancakes.
- **Serving Suggestion:** Serve with a side of scrambled eggs or fresh fruit for a complete meal.

Barbecue Bacon Pancakes offer a delicious combination of sweet and savory flavors that are sure to satisfy your taste buds. Enjoy this unique twist on traditional pancakes for a hearty breakfast or brunch!

Barbecue Chicken Pancakes

Ingredients:

For the Pancakes:

- 1 cup all-purpose flour
- 1 tablespoon granulated sugar
- 1 teaspoon baking powder
- 1/2 teaspoon baking soda
- Pinch of salt
- 1 cup buttermilk
- 1 large egg
- 2 tablespoons unsalted butter, melted
- Cooking spray or butter, for greasing the skillet

For the Barbecue Chicken:

- 2 cups cooked and shredded chicken (rotisserie chicken works well)
- 1/2 cup barbecue sauce (your favorite brand or homemade)
- 1/4 cup diced red onion (optional)
- 1/4 cup diced bell pepper (optional)
- Salt and pepper, to taste

For Serving:

- Additional barbecue sauce, for drizzling
- Chopped green onions or parsley, for garnish

Instructions:

1. **Prepare the Pancake Batter:**
    - In a large bowl, whisk together the flour, sugar, baking powder, baking soda, and salt.
    - In another bowl, whisk together the buttermilk, egg, and melted butter until smooth.
    - Pour the wet ingredients into the dry ingredients and stir until just combined. The batter should be slightly lumpy. Set aside.
2. **Prepare the Barbecue Chicken:**

- In a skillet over medium heat, combine the shredded chicken and barbecue sauce. Cook until heated through and the sauce coats the chicken evenly.
- If using, add diced red onion and bell pepper to the skillet. Cook for another 2-3 minutes until vegetables are softened. Season with salt and pepper to taste.

3. **Cook the Pancakes:**
    - Heat a non-stick skillet or griddle over medium heat. Lightly grease the surface with cooking spray or butter.
    - Pour about 1/4 cup of batter onto the skillet for each pancake. Cook until bubbles form on the surface of the pancake and the edges look set, about 2-3 minutes.
    - Flip the pancakes and cook for another 1-2 minutes, or until golden brown and cooked through.
    - Repeat with the remaining batter, adjusting the heat as needed.

4. **Assemble the Barbecue Chicken Pancakes:**
    - To assemble, place a pancake on a serving plate. Spread a layer of barbecue chicken mixture over the pancake.
    - Top with another pancake and repeat the layers until you have used all the pancakes and chicken mixture, ending with a pancake on top.

5. **Serve:**
    - Drizzle additional barbecue sauce over the top of the stack of pancakes.
    - Garnish with chopped green onions or parsley.
    - Serve Barbecue Chicken Pancakes warm as a hearty and flavorful meal.

Tips:

- **Variations:** Add shredded cheese or sliced avocado as additional toppings for extra flavor.
- **Make-Ahead:** You can prepare the barbecue chicken mixture ahead of time and store it in the refrigerator. Reheat before assembling the pancakes.
- **Serving Suggestion:** Serve with a side of coleslaw or a fresh green salad for a complete meal.

Barbecue Chicken Pancakes offer a delicious and savory twist on traditional pancakes, combining the hearty flavors of barbecue chicken with the fluffy texture of pancakes. Enjoy this unique dish for breakfast, brunch, or even dinner!

Anzac Biscuit Pancakes

Ingredients:

For the Pancakes:

- 1 cup all-purpose flour
- 1 tablespoon granulated sugar
- 1 teaspoon baking powder
- 1/2 teaspoon baking soda
- Pinch of salt
- 1 cup buttermilk
- 1 large egg
- 2 tablespoons unsalted butter, melted
- Cooking spray or butter, for greasing the skillet

For the Anzac Biscuit Crumble:

- 1/2 cup rolled oats
- 1/2 cup desiccated coconut
- 1/2 cup all-purpose flour
- 1/2 cup brown sugar
- 1/4 cup unsalted butter, melted
- 2 tablespoons golden syrup or honey
- 1/2 teaspoon baking soda
- 1 tablespoon boiling water

For Serving:

- Maple syrup or golden syrup, for drizzling
- Whipped cream or vanilla ice cream, for topping (optional)

Instructions:

1. **Prepare the Anzac Biscuit Crumble:**
    - Preheat your oven to 180°C (350°F). Line a baking sheet with parchment paper.
    - In a large bowl, combine the rolled oats, desiccated coconut, flour, and brown sugar.
    - In a separate bowl, mix together the melted butter and golden syrup or honey.

- Dissolve the baking soda in boiling water, then add it to the butter mixture.
- Pour the wet ingredients into the dry ingredients and mix until well combined and crumbly.
- Spread the mixture evenly onto the prepared baking sheet.
- Bake for 10-12 minutes, or until golden brown and crisp. Remove from the oven and let it cool completely. Once cooled, break the crumble into small pieces.

2. **Prepare the Pancake Batter:**
   - In a large bowl, whisk together the flour, sugar, baking powder, baking soda, and salt.
   - In another bowl, whisk together the buttermilk, egg, and melted butter until smooth.
   - Pour the wet ingredients into the dry ingredients and stir until just combined. The batter should be slightly lumpy. Set aside.

3. **Cook the Pancakes:**
   - Heat a non-stick skillet or griddle over medium heat. Lightly grease the surface with cooking spray or butter.
   - Pour about 1/4 cup of batter onto the skillet for each pancake. Cook until bubbles form on the surface of the pancake and the edges look set, about 2-3 minutes.
   - Flip the pancakes and cook for another 1-2 minutes, or until golden brown and cooked through.
   - Repeat with the remaining batter, adjusting the heat as needed.

4. **Assemble Anzac Biscuit Pancakes:**
   - To assemble, stack the pancakes on a serving plate.
   - Sprinkle a generous amount of Anzac biscuit crumble over each pancake stack.

5. **Serve:**
   - Drizzle with maple syrup or golden syrup.
   - Optionally, top with whipped cream or a scoop of vanilla ice cream.
   - Serve Anzac Biscuit Pancakes warm as a delightful and comforting breakfast or dessert.

Tips:

- **Make-Ahead:** You can prepare the Anzac biscuit crumble ahead of time and store it in an airtight container at room temperature.
- **Variations:** Add a sprinkle of chopped nuts or dried fruits to the Anzac biscuit crumble for extra texture and flavor.

- **Presentation:** Garnish with fresh berries or mint leaves for a pop of color and freshness.

Anzac Biscuit Pancakes offer a delightful fusion of classic Anzac biscuit flavors with fluffy pancakes, making them a perfect treat for any occasion. Enjoy these comforting pancakes for a special breakfast or dessert!

Anzac Biscuit Toast

Ingredients:

- 4 slices of bread (white, whole wheat, or your preferred type)
- 1/2 cup rolled oats
- 1/2 cup desiccated coconut
- 1/2 cup all-purpose flour
- 1/2 cup brown sugar
- 1/4 cup unsalted butter, melted
- 2 tablespoons golden syrup or honey
- 1/2 teaspoon baking soda
- 1 tablespoon boiling water

Instructions:

1. **Prepare the Anzac Biscuit Topping:**
    - Preheat your oven to 180°C (350°F). Line a baking sheet with parchment paper.
    - In a large bowl, combine the rolled oats, desiccated coconut, flour, and brown sugar.
    - In a separate bowl, mix together the melted butter and golden syrup or honey.
    - Dissolve the baking soda in boiling water, then add it to the butter mixture.
    - Pour the wet ingredients into the dry ingredients and mix until well combined and crumbly.
    - Spread the mixture evenly onto the prepared baking sheet.
    - Bake for 10-12 minutes, or until golden brown and crisp. Remove from the oven and let it cool completely. Once cooled, break the crumble into small pieces.
2. **Prepare the Toast:**
    - Toast the bread slices until golden brown and crispy. You can use a toaster or toast them in a skillet with a bit of butter for extra flavor.
3. **Assemble Anzac Biscuit Toast:**
    - Spread a generous amount of butter on each toasted bread slice while they are still warm.
    - Sprinkle a layer of the Anzac biscuit crumble over the buttered toast slices, pressing gently to adhere the crumble.
4. **Serve:**
    - Serve Anzac Biscuit Toast warm as a delicious breakfast or snack.

Tips:

- **Storage:** Store any leftover Anzac biscuit crumble in an airtight container at room temperature for up to a week.
- **Variations:** Drizzle honey or golden syrup over the Anzac Biscuit Toast for extra sweetness.
- **Presentation:** Garnish with a dusting of powdered sugar or a sprinkle of cinnamon for added flavor.

Anzac Biscuit Toast offers a delightful blend of crunchy Anzac biscuit topping with warm, buttery toast, making it a perfect treat for any time of day. Enjoy this unique twist on a classic Australian favorite!

Pavlova Pancakes

Ingredients:

For the Pancakes:

- 1 cup all-purpose flour
- 1 tablespoon granulated sugar
- 1 teaspoon baking powder
- 1/2 teaspoon baking soda
- Pinch of salt
- 1 cup buttermilk
- 1 large egg
- 2 tablespoons unsalted butter, melted
- Cooking spray or butter, for greasing the skillet

For the Pavlova Topping:

- 1 cup whipped cream
- Fresh fruits (such as strawberries, kiwi, berries, or mango), sliced
- 1/4 cup raspberry jam or fruit compote
- 2 tablespoons powdered sugar, for dusting (optional)
- Mint leaves, for garnish (optional)

Instructions:

1. **Prepare the Pancake Batter:**
    - In a large bowl, whisk together the flour, sugar, baking powder, baking soda, and salt.
    - In another bowl, whisk together the buttermilk, egg, and melted butter until smooth.
    - Pour the wet ingredients into the dry ingredients and stir until just combined. The batter should be slightly lumpy. Set aside.
2. **Cook the Pancakes:**
    - Heat a non-stick skillet or griddle over medium heat. Lightly grease the surface with cooking spray or butter.
    - Pour about 1/4 cup of batter onto the skillet for each pancake. Cook until bubbles form on the surface of the pancake and the edges look set, about 2-3 minutes.
    - Flip the pancakes and cook for another 1-2 minutes, or until golden brown and cooked through.

- Repeat with the remaining batter, adjusting the heat as needed.
3. **Prepare the Pavlova Topping:**
   - In a bowl, whip the cream until stiff peaks form.
   - Spread a layer of whipped cream over each pancake.
   - Arrange the sliced fresh fruits over the whipped cream.
   - Spoon a dollop of raspberry jam or fruit compote over the fruits.
4. **Serve:**
   - Dust the Pavlova Pancakes with powdered sugar, if desired.
   - Garnish with mint leaves for a fresh touch.
   - Serve Pavlova Pancakes immediately as a delightful and decadent breakfast or brunch dish.

Tips:

- **Variations:** Add a sprinkle of toasted nuts or shredded coconut for extra texture.
- **Make-Ahead:** You can prepare the pancake batter and cook the pancakes ahead of time. Store the cooked pancakes in a single layer on a baking sheet, covered with foil, and reheat them in a low oven before serving.
- **Serving Suggestion:** Serve with extra whipped cream or a scoop of vanilla ice cream for an indulgent treat.

Pavlova Pancakes offer a delightful fusion of fluffy pancakes with the fresh and fruity flavors of Pavlova, making them a perfect dish for a special breakfast or brunch. Enjoy this unique twist on a classic dessert!

Anzac Biscuit Waffles

Ingredients:

For the Anzac Biscuit Waffles:

- 1 cup all-purpose flour
- 1/2 cup rolled oats
- 1/2 cup desiccated coconut
- 1/2 cup brown sugar
- 1/2 teaspoon baking powder
- 1/2 teaspoon baking soda
- Pinch of salt
- 1/2 cup unsalted butter, melted
- 2 tablespoons golden syrup or honey
- 1 teaspoon vanilla extract
- 1/4 cup milk
- 2 large eggs

For Serving:

- Maple syrup or golden syrup
- Whipped cream or vanilla ice cream (optional)
- Fresh berries or sliced bananas (optional)

Instructions:

1. **Prepare the Anzac Biscuit Waffle Batter:**
   - Preheat your waffle iron according to manufacturer's instructions.
   - In a large bowl, combine the flour, rolled oats, desiccated coconut, brown sugar, baking powder, baking soda, and salt.
   - In another bowl, whisk together the melted butter, golden syrup or honey, vanilla extract, milk, and eggs until well combined.
   - Pour the wet ingredients into the dry ingredients and stir until just combined. The batter should be thick and slightly lumpy.
2. **Cook the Waffles:**
   - Lightly grease the waffle iron with non-stick cooking spray or melted butter.
   - Spoon the batter onto the preheated waffle iron, spreading it evenly. Close the lid and cook according to your waffle iron's instructions until golden brown and crisp.

- Transfer the cooked waffles to a wire rack to cool slightly while you prepare the remaining waffles.
3. **Serve Anzac Biscuit Waffles:**
    - Drizzle warm maple syrup or golden syrup over the waffles.
    - Optionally, top with whipped cream or a scoop of vanilla ice cream.
    - Garnish with fresh berries or sliced bananas, if desired.
    - Serve Anzac Biscuit Waffles warm as a delicious breakfast or dessert.

Tips:

- **Storage:** Waffles can be stored in an airtight container in the refrigerator for up to 3 days or frozen for up to 1 month. Reheat in a toaster or toaster oven until warmed through.
- **Variations:** Add a sprinkle of chopped nuts or chocolate chips to the waffle batter for extra flavor and texture.
- **Make-Ahead:** You can prepare the waffle batter the night before and refrigerate it. Stir well before using it the next morning.

Anzac Biscuit Waffles offer a delightful combination of crunchy oats and coconut with the fluffy texture of waffles, perfect for a special breakfast or brunch treat. Enjoy these unique waffles with your favorite toppings for a memorable meal!

Kangaroo Sausage Roll

Ingredients:

For the Filling:

- 500g kangaroo mince
- 1 onion, finely chopped
- 1 garlic clove, minced
- 1 tablespoon olive oil
- 1/2 cup breadcrumbs
- 1 egg
- 1 tablespoon Worcestershire sauce
- Salt and pepper, to taste
- 2 tablespoons chopped parsley (optional)

For the Pastry:

- 1-2 sheets of ready-rolled puff pastry
- 1 egg, beaten (for egg wash)

Instructions:

1. **Prepare the Filling:**
    - Preheat your oven to 200°C (400°F) and line a baking tray with parchment paper.
    - In a frying pan, heat the olive oil over medium heat. Add the chopped onion and minced garlic, and cook until softened and lightly golden.
    - In a large bowl, combine the kangaroo mince, cooked onion and garlic mixture, breadcrumbs, egg, Worcestershire sauce, salt, pepper, and chopped parsley (if using). Mix well until thoroughly combined.
2. **Assemble the Sausage Rolls:**
    - Roll out the puff pastry sheets on a lightly floured surface. Cut each sheet in half lengthwise to create two long rectangles.
    - Divide the kangaroo mince mixture into equal portions and shape each portion into a long sausage shape, slightly shorter than the length of the pastry.
    - Place each portion of kangaroo mince along the center of each pastry rectangle.
    - Brush one edge of the pastry with beaten egg. Roll the pastry over the filling, sealing the edge with the egg-washed edge.

- Place the sausage rolls seam-side down on the prepared baking tray.
3. **Bake the Sausage Rolls:**
    - Brush the tops of the sausage rolls with more beaten egg to create a golden crust when baked.
    - Using a sharp knife, make small slits on the tops of each sausage roll to allow steam to escape.
    - Bake in the preheated oven for 20-25 minutes, or until the pastry is golden brown and crisp, and the filling is cooked through.
4. **Serve:**
    - Remove from the oven and let the Kangaroo Sausage Rolls cool slightly on a wire rack.
    - Serve warm as a delicious snack or meal, accompanied by tomato sauce or your favorite dipping sauce.

Tips:

- **Variations:** Add grated cheese or finely chopped herbs to the kangaroo mince mixture for extra flavor.
- **Make-Ahead:** You can assemble the Kangaroo Sausage Rolls ahead of time and refrigerate them until ready to bake. Brush with egg wash just before baking.
- **Freezing:** These sausage rolls freeze well. After baking, let them cool completely, then wrap tightly in foil or plastic wrap and freeze for up to 3 months. Reheat in the oven until heated through.

Kangaroo Sausage Rolls offer a unique twist on the traditional sausage roll, showcasing the lean and flavorful kangaroo meat wrapped in crispy puff pastry. Enjoy these savory treats for a taste of Australian cuisine!

Pavlova Waffles

Ingredients:

For the Waffles:

- 1 cup all-purpose flour
- 1 tablespoon granulated sugar
- 1 teaspoon baking powder
- 1/2 teaspoon baking soda
- Pinch of salt
- 1 cup buttermilk
- 1 large egg
- 2 tablespoons unsalted butter, melted
- Cooking spray or butter, for greasing the waffle iron

For the Pavlova Topping:

- 1 cup whipped cream
- Fresh fruits (such as strawberries, kiwi, berries, or mango), sliced
- 1/4 cup raspberry jam or fruit compote
- 2 tablespoons powdered sugar, for dusting (optional)
- Mint leaves, for garnish (optional)

Instructions:

1. **Prepare the Waffle Batter:**
    - Preheat your waffle iron according to manufacturer's instructions.
    - In a large bowl, whisk together the flour, sugar, baking powder, baking soda, and salt.
    - In another bowl, whisk together the buttermilk, egg, and melted butter until smooth.
    - Pour the wet ingredients into the dry ingredients and stir until just combined. The batter should be slightly lumpy.
2. **Cook the Waffles:**
    - Lightly grease the waffle iron with cooking spray or melted butter.
    - Spoon the batter onto the preheated waffle iron, spreading it evenly. Close the lid and cook according to your waffle iron's instructions until golden brown and crisp.
    - Transfer the cooked waffles to a wire rack to cool slightly while you prepare the remaining waffles.

3. **Prepare the Pavlova Topping:**
    - In a bowl, whip the cream until stiff peaks form.
    - Spread a layer of whipped cream over each waffle.
    - Arrange the sliced fresh fruits over the whipped cream.
    - Spoon a dollop of raspberry jam or fruit compote over the fruits.
4. **Serve:**
    - Dust the Pavlova Waffles with powdered sugar, if desired.
    - Garnish with mint leaves for a fresh touch.
    - Serve Pavlova Waffles immediately as a delightful and decadent breakfast or brunch dish.

Tips:

- **Storage:** Waffles can be stored in an airtight container in the refrigerator for up to 3 days or frozen for up to 1 month. Reheat in a toaster or toaster oven until warmed through.
- **Variations:** Add a sprinkle of toasted nuts or shredded coconut for extra texture and flavor.
- **Make-Ahead:** You can prepare the waffle batter the night before and refrigerate it. Stir well before using it the next morning.

Pavlova Waffles offer a delightful combination of crispy waffles topped with fluffy whipped cream and fresh fruits, reminiscent of the beloved Pavlova dessert. Enjoy these unique waffles for a special breakfast or brunch treat!

Pineapple and Coconut Smoothie Bowl

Ingredients:

For the Smoothie Base:

- 1 cup frozen pineapple chunks
- 1/2 cup coconut milk (canned, full-fat for creaminess)
- 1 ripe banana, frozen
- 1/4 cup Greek yogurt
- 1 tablespoon honey (optional, for added sweetness)
- Juice of 1/2 lime (optional, for a tangy twist)

For Toppings:

- Fresh pineapple slices
- Shredded coconut
- Granola
- Chia seeds
- Sliced bananas
- Fresh berries (optional)

Instructions:

1. **Prepare the Smoothie Base:**
    - In a blender, combine the frozen pineapple chunks, coconut milk, frozen banana, Greek yogurt, honey (if using), and lime juice (if using).
    - Blend until smooth and creamy. If the mixture is too thick, you can add a splash of additional coconut milk or water to reach your desired consistency.
2. **Assemble the Smoothie Bowl:**
    - Pour the smoothie base into a bowl.
3. **Add Toppings:**
    - Arrange fresh pineapple slices, shredded coconut, granola, chia seeds, sliced bananas, and any other desired toppings over the smoothie bowl.
4. **Serve:**
    - Serve the Pineapple and Coconut Smoothie Bowl immediately.

Tips:

- **Variations:** You can add spinach or kale for a green boost without altering the taste too much. Adding a scoop of protein powder can also increase the protein content.
- **Make-Ahead:** Prepare the smoothie base in advance and store it in an airtight container in the refrigerator. When ready to serve, simply pour into a bowl and add your toppings.
- **Customize:** Feel free to customize your toppings based on personal preference and what you have on hand.

Pineapple and Coconut Smoothie Bowl offers a tropical and nutritious breakfast or snack option, packed with vitamins, fiber, and natural sweetness. Enjoy the refreshing flavors and textures of this smoothie bowl to kick-start your day!

Chia Seed Pudding with Berries

Ingredients:

- 1/4 cup chia seeds
- 1 cup milk (dairy milk, almond milk, coconut milk, or any milk of your choice)
- 1 tablespoon honey or maple syrup (optional, for sweetness)
- 1/2 teaspoon vanilla extract (optional, for flavor)
- Fresh berries (such as strawberries, blueberries, raspberries)
- Sliced fruits (optional, such as banana or kiwi)
- Nuts or granola for topping (optional)

Instructions:

1. **Prepare the Chia Seed Pudding:**
   - In a bowl or jar, combine the chia seeds, milk, honey or maple syrup (if using), and vanilla extract (if using). Stir well to combine.
   - Cover the bowl or jar and refrigerate for at least 2 hours or overnight. Stir or shake occasionally during the first hour to prevent clumping.
2. **Assemble the Chia Seed Pudding with Berries:**
   - Once the chia seeds have absorbed the liquid and thickened to a pudding-like consistency, remove from the refrigerator.
3. **Serve:**
   - Spoon the chia seed pudding into serving bowls or jars.
   - Top with fresh berries, sliced fruits, nuts, or granola.
   - Serve chilled and enjoy immediately.

Tips:

- **Sweeteners:** Adjust the sweetness level by adding more or less honey or maple syrup according to your preference.
- **Milk Options:** You can use any type of milk you prefer—dairy milk, almond milk, coconut milk, etc. Each type will lend a slightly different flavor and consistency to the pudding.
- **Toppings:** Feel free to customize your chia seed pudding with various toppings such as additional fruits, nuts, seeds, or a drizzle of honey or yogurt.

Chia Seed Pudding with Berries is not only delicious but also packed with fiber, omega-3 fatty acids, and antioxidants from the chia seeds and fresh berries. It's a nutritious and satisfying option for any time of day!

Acai Bowl with Granola

Ingredients:

- 2 packets of frozen unsweetened acai puree (available in most grocery stores or online)
- 1 banana, frozen
- 1/2 cup frozen mixed berries (such as strawberries, blueberries, raspberries)
- 1/2 cup milk (dairy milk, almond milk, coconut milk, or any milk of your choice)
- 1 tablespoon honey or maple syrup (optional, for sweetness)
- Toppings:
    - Granola
    - Fresh fruits (such as sliced bananas, berries, kiwi)
    - Chia seeds
    - Shredded coconut
    - Nuts or seeds (such as almonds, walnuts, sunflower seeds)
    - Drizzle of honey or agave syrup (optional)

Instructions:

1. **Prepare the Acai Bowl Base:**
    - In a blender, combine the frozen acai puree packets, frozen banana, frozen mixed berries, milk, and honey or maple syrup (if using).
    - Blend until smooth and creamy, scraping down the sides of the blender as needed to ensure all ingredients are well combined.
2. **Assemble the Acai Bowl:**
    - Pour the blended acai mixture into a bowl.
3. **Add Toppings:**
    - Sprinkle granola generously over the top of the acai mixture.
    - Arrange fresh fruits, chia seeds, shredded coconut, and nuts or seeds on top of the granola.
4. **Serve:**
    - Drizzle with honey or agave syrup, if desired.
    - Serve the Acai Bowl immediately with a spoon and enjoy!

Tips:

- **Variations:** Feel free to customize your Acai Bowl with different toppings such as yogurt, nut butter, cacao nibs, or dried fruits.

- **Sweeteners:** Adjust the sweetness level by adding more or less honey or maple syrup according to your preference.
- **Texture:** The key to a satisfying Acai Bowl is the contrast in textures—creamy acai base, crunchy granola, and fresh fruits.
- **Make-Ahead:** You can prepare the acai mixture in advance and store it covered in the refrigerator for up to a day. Assemble with toppings just before serving.

Acai Bowl with Granola is not only visually appealing but also packed with antioxidants, vitamins, and fiber, making it a perfect breakfast or snack option for a healthy start to your day!

Grilled Veggie Breakfast Wrap

Ingredients:

- 1 large whole wheat or spinach tortilla wrap
- 1/2 cup sliced bell peppers (any color)
- 1/2 cup sliced mushrooms
- 1/2 cup sliced zucchini or squash
- 1/4 cup sliced red onion
- 1 tablespoon olive oil
- Salt and pepper, to taste
- 2 large eggs
- 1/4 cup shredded cheese (such as cheddar or mozzarella)
- Fresh spinach leaves or mixed greens
- Salsa or hot sauce (optional)
- Avocado slices (optional)

Instructions:

1. **Prepare the Grilled Vegetables:**
    - Heat olive oil in a skillet over medium-high heat.
    - Add sliced bell peppers, mushrooms, zucchini or squash, and red onion to the skillet.
    - Season with salt and pepper to taste.
    - Cook, stirring occasionally, until the vegetables are tender and slightly caramelized, about 5-7 minutes. Remove from heat and set aside.
2. **Prepare the Eggs:**
    - In the same skillet (after removing the vegetables), crack the eggs and cook them according to your preference (scrambled, fried, or as an omelette).
    - Once cooked, sprinkle shredded cheese over the eggs and allow it to melt slightly.
3. **Assemble the Breakfast Wrap:**
    - Warm the tortilla wrap slightly in a separate skillet or microwave, if desired.
    - Place fresh spinach leaves or mixed greens on the tortilla wrap.
    - Spoon the grilled vegetables onto the greens, followed by the cheesy eggs.
    - Optionally, add salsa or hot sauce for extra flavor and avocado slices for creaminess.
4. **Wrap and Serve:**

- Fold the sides of the tortilla towards the center, then roll it up tightly from the bottom to enclose the fillings.
- Slice the wrap in half diagonally, if desired, and serve immediately.

Tips:

- **Variations:** You can customize your Grilled Veggie Breakfast Wrap with additional ingredients such as black beans, diced tomatoes, or cooked quinoa.
- **Make-Ahead:** Prepare the grilled vegetables and cook the eggs ahead of time. Assemble the wrap just before serving to ensure it stays fresh and warm.
- **Protein Boost:** Add a few slices of cooked bacon or turkey sausage for extra protein.

Grilled Veggie Breakfast Wrap is a satisfying and nutritious meal that's perfect for a quick and wholesome breakfast on the go. Enjoy the flavors of grilled vegetables and eggs wrapped in a warm tortilla for a delicious start to your day!

Caramelized Banana Pancakes

Ingredients:

For the Pancakes:

- 1 cup all-purpose flour
- 2 tablespoons granulated sugar
- 1 teaspoon baking powder
- 1/2 teaspoon baking soda
- Pinch of salt
- 1 cup buttermilk
- 1 large egg
- 2 tablespoons unsalted butter, melted
- Cooking spray or additional butter, for cooking

For the Caramelized Banana Topping:

- 2 ripe bananas, sliced
- 2 tablespoons unsalted butter
- 2 tablespoons brown sugar
- Pinch of cinnamon (optional)
- Pinch of salt

Optional Garnishes:

- Chopped nuts (such as walnuts or pecans)
- Whipped cream or vanilla yogurt
- Maple syrup

Instructions:

1. **Prepare the Pancake Batter:**
    - In a large bowl, whisk together the flour, sugar, baking powder, baking soda, and salt.
    - In another bowl, whisk together the buttermilk, egg, and melted butter until smooth.
    - Pour the wet ingredients into the dry ingredients and stir until just combined. The batter should be slightly lumpy. Set aside.
2. **Make the Caramelized Banana Topping:**
    - In a skillet, melt the butter over medium heat.

- Add the sliced bananas and cook for 1-2 minutes, stirring gently.
- Sprinkle the brown sugar, cinnamon (if using), and salt over the bananas. Continue cooking, stirring occasionally, until the bananas are caramelized and golden brown, about 3-4 minutes. Remove from heat and set aside.

3. **Cook the Pancakes:**
   - Heat a non-stick skillet or griddle over medium heat. Lightly grease the surface with cooking spray or melted butter.
   - Pour about 1/4 cup of batter onto the skillet for each pancake. Cook until bubbles form on the surface of the pancake and the edges look set, about 2-3 minutes.
   - Flip the pancakes and cook for another 1-2 minutes, or until golden brown and cooked through.
   - Transfer the cooked pancakes to a plate and cover with foil to keep warm while you cook the remaining pancakes.

4. **Assemble the Caramelized Banana Pancakes:**
   - Stack the pancakes on serving plates.
   - Spoon the caramelized banana mixture over the top of each pancake stack.

5. **Serve:**
   - Garnish with chopped nuts, whipped cream or yogurt, and a drizzle of maple syrup, if desired.
   - Serve Caramelized Banana Pancakes warm as a delicious and indulgent breakfast treat.

Tips:

- **Variations:** Add a splash of rum or vanilla extract to the caramelized bananas for extra flavor.
- **Make-Ahead:** You can prepare the pancake batter and caramelized bananas ahead of time. Store the pancakes in a warm oven (about 200°F) until ready to serve.
- **Storage:** Leftover pancakes can be stored in an airtight container in the refrigerator for up to 2 days. Reheat in a toaster or toaster oven until warmed through.

Caramelized Banana Pancakes are a decadent and flavorful twist on classic pancakes, perfect for a special breakfast or brunch. Enjoy the combination of fluffy pancakes with sweet, caramelized bananas for a memorable meal!

Australian Meat Pie

Ingredients:

For the Pie Filling:

- 500g ground beef or lamb
- 1 onion, finely chopped
- 2 garlic cloves, minced
- 1 carrot, finely diced
- 1 celery stalk, finely diced
- 1 tablespoon tomato paste
- 1 cup beef or vegetable broth
- 1 tablespoon Worcestershire sauce
- 1 tablespoon soy sauce
- Salt and pepper, to taste
- 2 tablespoons olive oil
- 2 tablespoons all-purpose flour (optional, for thickening)

For the Pastry:

- 2 sheets of pre-made shortcrust pastry (for the base)
- 2 sheets of pre-made puff pastry (for the top)
- 1 egg, beaten (for egg wash)

Instructions:

1. **Prepare the Pie Filling:**
    - Heat olive oil in a large skillet or frying pan over medium heat.
    - Add the chopped onion and minced garlic. Cook until softened and translucent, about 3-4 minutes.
    - Add the ground beef or lamb to the skillet. Cook, breaking up the meat with a spoon, until browned and cooked through.
    - Stir in the diced carrot and celery. Cook for another 3-4 minutes until vegetables are softened.
    - Add tomato paste, Worcestershire sauce, soy sauce, salt, and pepper. Stir to combine.
    - If desired, sprinkle flour over the mixture and stir well to incorporate. This will help thicken the filling.
    - Pour in the beef or vegetable broth, stirring constantly until the mixture thickens slightly. Simmer for about 10-15 minutes until the filling is thick

and flavors have melded together. Remove from heat and set aside to cool slightly.
2. **Prepare the Pastry and Assemble:**
    - Preheat your oven to 200°C (400°F). Line a baking tray with parchment paper.
    - Roll out the shortcrust pastry sheets on a lightly floured surface. Use a round cutter or a bowl to cut out circles that will fit your pie molds or ramekins.
    - Line the base and sides of each pie mold or ramekin with the shortcrust pastry circles.
    - Fill each pastry-lined mold with the cooled meat filling.
    - Roll out the puff pastry sheets and cut out circles slightly larger than the tops of your pie molds or ramekins.
    - Brush the edges of the pastry in the molds with beaten egg. Place the puff pastry circles over the top of each pie mold, pressing down gently to seal the edges.
    - Use a fork to crimp the edges of the pastry together. Brush the tops of the pies with beaten egg for a golden finish.
3. **Bake the Pies:**
    - Place the assembled pies on the prepared baking tray.
    - Bake in the preheated oven for 20-25 minutes, or until the pastry is golden brown and crisp.
    - Remove from the oven and let the pies cool slightly before serving.
4. **Serve:**
    - Australian Meat Pies are traditionally served hot with tomato sauce (ketchup) or your favorite condiments.

Tips:

- **Variations:** You can customize the filling by adding mushrooms, peas, or other vegetables of your choice.
- **Make-Ahead:** You can prepare the pie filling ahead of time and store it in the refrigerator for up to 2 days. Assemble and bake the pies when ready to serve.
- **Freezing:** Baked meat pies can be frozen for up to 3 months. Reheat in the oven until heated through.

Australian Meat Pies are a delicious and hearty meal, perfect for any occasion. Enjoy the rich flavors and flaky pastry of these iconic pies straight from Down Under!

Healthy Breakfast Burrito

Ingredients:

- 4 large whole wheat tortillas (or your preferred tortilla type)
- 4 large eggs
- 1/2 cup diced bell peppers (any color)
- 1/2 cup diced tomatoes
- 1/4 cup diced red onion
- 1 cup fresh spinach leaves
- 1/2 cup black beans, drained and rinsed
- 1/2 cup shredded cheddar cheese (optional)
- Salt and pepper, to taste
- Cooking spray or olive oil

Optional Additions/Toppings:

- Avocado slices or guacamole
- Salsa or pico de gallo
- Greek yogurt or sour cream
- Fresh cilantro, chopped
- Hot sauce or jalapeños

Instructions:

1. **Prepare the Eggs:**
    - In a bowl, whisk the eggs until well combined. Season with salt and pepper to taste.
    - Heat a non-stick skillet over medium heat and spray with cooking spray or add a drizzle of olive oil.
    - Pour the whisked eggs into the skillet and cook, stirring gently, until scrambled and cooked through. Remove from heat and set aside.
2. **Prepare the Burrito Filling:**
    - In the same skillet (or a separate one), add diced bell peppers, tomatoes, and red onion. Cook over medium heat until vegetables are softened, about 3-4 minutes.
    - Add fresh spinach leaves to the skillet and cook for another 1-2 minutes until wilted.
    - Stir in black beans and cooked scrambled eggs. Mix well to combine. If using shredded cheese, add it at this point and stir until melted.
3. **Assemble the Breakfast Burritos:**

- Warm the tortillas slightly in the microwave or a dry skillet to make them easier to fold.
- Spoon the filling onto the center of each tortilla.
- Add any optional toppings or additions, such as avocado slices, salsa, Greek yogurt, or fresh cilantro.

4. **Wrap the Burritos:**
   - Fold the sides of each tortilla towards the center, then roll it up tightly from the bottom to enclose the filling.
   - For a secure wrap, you can tuck the sides in as you roll.
5. **Serve:**
   - Serve the Healthy Breakfast Burritos immediately, whole or sliced in half diagonally.

Tips:

- **Make-Ahead:** You can prepare the burrito filling ahead of time and store it in the refrigerator for up to 3 days. Reheat before assembling the burritos.
- **Variations:** Customize your Healthy Breakfast Burrito with different vegetables, such as mushrooms or spinach. You can also add cooked quinoa or brown rice for added fiber and protein.
- **Freezing:** Wrapped burritos can be frozen for up to 2 months. To reheat, thaw overnight in the refrigerator and then heat in the microwave or oven until warmed through.

Healthy Breakfast Burritos are a convenient and nutritious option for busy mornings. Packed with protein, fiber, and vitamins, they provide a satisfying start to your day!

Kiwi and Mango Smoothie

Ingredients:

- 1 ripe mango, peeled, seeded, and chopped
- 2 ripe kiwis, peeled and chopped
- 1 banana, peeled and sliced (frozen banana works well too)
- 1 cup spinach leaves (optional, for added nutrients)
- 1 cup plain Greek yogurt or coconut yogurt
- 1/2 cup coconut water or almond milk (adjust to desired consistency)
- 1 tablespoon honey or maple syrup (optional, for added sweetness)
- Ice cubes (optional, for a chilled smoothie)

Instructions:

1. **Prepare the Ingredients:**
    - Peel and chop the mango and kiwis.
    - Slice the banana. If using fresh banana and prefer a colder smoothie, freeze the banana slices beforehand.
2. **Blend the Smoothie:**
    - In a blender, combine the chopped mango, kiwis, banana slices, spinach leaves (if using), Greek yogurt or coconut yogurt, and coconut water or almond milk.
    - Add honey or maple syrup, if using, for extra sweetness.
    - Optionally, add ice cubes for a colder smoothie and blend until smooth and creamy.
3. **Adjust Consistency:**
    - If the smoothie is too thick, add more coconut water or almond milk, a little at a time, until you reach your desired consistency.
4. **Serve:**
    - Pour the Kiwi and Mango Smoothie into glasses.
    - Garnish with slices of kiwi or mango, if desired.
    - Serve immediately and enjoy the refreshing flavors!

Tips:

- **Variations:** Add a handful of fresh mint leaves or a squeeze of lime juice for a zesty twist. You can also substitute spinach with kale or other leafy greens.
- **Protein Boost:** Add a scoop of protein powder or chia seeds for added protein and nutrients.

- **Make-Ahead:** You can prepare the ingredients ahead of time and store them in the refrigerator until ready to blend.

Kiwi and Mango Smoothie is a delicious blend of tropical fruits that's packed with vitamins, fiber, and antioxidants. It's perfect for a quick breakfast or a refreshing snack any time of the day!

Barramundi Breakfast Tacos

Ingredients:

- 2 barramundi fillets, skinless
- 1 tablespoon olive oil
- Salt and pepper, to taste
- 1 teaspoon ground cumin
- 1 teaspoon paprika
- 1/2 teaspoon garlic powder
- 1/2 teaspoon onion powder
- 4-6 small corn or flour tortillas
- 4 large eggs
- 1 avocado, sliced
- Fresh salsa or pico de gallo
- Fresh cilantro, chopped (optional)
- Lime wedges (optional, for serving)

Instructions:

1. **Prepare the Barramundi:**
   - Pat dry the barramundi fillets with paper towels to remove excess moisture.
   - In a small bowl, mix together salt, pepper, ground cumin, paprika, garlic powder, and onion powder.
   - Rub the spice mixture evenly over both sides of the barramundi fillets.
   - Heat olive oil in a skillet over medium-high heat. Cook the barramundi fillets for 3-4 minutes on each side, or until cooked through and flaky. Remove from heat and let rest for a few minutes. Flake the barramundi into bite-sized pieces.
2. **Prepare the Tortillas:**
   - Warm the tortillas in a dry skillet over medium heat for about 30 seconds on each side, or until warmed through and slightly charred. Alternatively, warm them in the microwave according to package instructions.
3. **Cook the Eggs:**
   - In the same skillet used for the barramundi (or a separate skillet), crack the eggs and cook them according to your preference (scrambled, fried, or as an omelette).
4. **Assemble the Tacos:**

- Divide the cooked barramundi and scrambled eggs evenly among the warmed tortillas.
- Top each taco with slices of avocado, fresh salsa or pico de gallo, and chopped cilantro, if using.

5. **Serve:**
   - Serve Barramundi Breakfast Tacos immediately, with lime wedges on the side for squeezing over the tacos, if desired.

Tips:

- **Variations:** Customize your tacos with additional toppings such as shredded cheese, sour cream or Greek yogurt, jalapeño slices, or hot sauce.
- **Make-Ahead:** Cook the barramundi ahead of time and store it in an airtight container in the refrigerator. Reheat gently before assembling the tacos.
- **Substitutions:** If barramundi is not available, you can use other mild-flavored fish such as cod or tilapia.

Barramundi Breakfast Tacos are a flavorful and protein-packed breakfast option that combines the goodness of fish with the versatility of tacos. Enjoy these delicious tacos to kick-start your day with a satisfying meal!

Ricotta Hotcakes with Honeycomb Butter

Ingredients:

For the Ricotta Hotcakes:

- 1 cup ricotta cheese
- 3/4 cup milk
- 2 large eggs, separated
- 1 teaspoon vanilla extract
- 1 cup all-purpose flour
- 1 tablespoon sugar
- 1 teaspoon baking powder
- 1/2 teaspoon baking soda
- Pinch of salt
- Butter or oil, for cooking

For the Honeycomb Butter:

- 1/2 cup unsalted butter, softened
- 2 tablespoons honey
- 1/2 teaspoon vanilla extract
- Pinch of sea salt (optional)

Instructions:

1. **Prepare the Honeycomb Butter:**
    - In a small bowl, combine softened butter, honey, vanilla extract, and a pinch of sea salt (if using). Mix until well combined.
    - Transfer the honeycomb butter mixture onto a sheet of plastic wrap or parchment paper. Roll into a log shape and twist the ends to seal. Refrigerate until firm.
2. **Prepare the Ricotta Hotcakes:**
    - In a large bowl, whisk together ricotta cheese, milk, egg yolks, and vanilla extract until smooth.
    - In a separate bowl, sift together flour, sugar, baking powder, baking soda, and salt.
    - Gradually add the dry ingredients to the ricotta mixture, stirring until just combined. Do not overmix.
    - In another clean bowl, beat the egg whites until stiff peaks form.

- Gently fold the beaten egg whites into the ricotta batter using a spatula, until just incorporated.
3. **Cook the Hotcakes:**
   - Heat a large non-stick skillet or griddle over medium heat. Add a small amount of butter or oil to coat the surface.
   - Pour 1/4 cup of batter onto the skillet for each hotcake, spreading slightly with the back of a spoon to form a round shape.
   - Cook until bubbles form on the surface of the hotcakes and the edges look set, about 2-3 minutes.
   - Flip the hotcakes and cook for another 1-2 minutes, or until golden brown and cooked through.
   - Transfer cooked hotcakes to a plate and keep warm. Repeat with the remaining batter.
4. **Serve:**
   - Serve Ricotta Hotcakes warm, topped with slices of honeycomb butter.
   - Optionally, drizzle with additional honey or maple syrup.

Tips:

- **Variations:** You can add lemon zest or blueberries to the batter for extra flavor.
- **Make-Ahead:** The honeycomb butter can be made ahead of time and stored in the refrigerator. The hotcakes can also be cooked ahead and reheated in a toaster oven.
- **Presentation:** Garnish with fresh berries, a dusting of powdered sugar, or a dollop of whipped cream for an extra special presentation.

Ricotta Hotcakes with Honeycomb Butter are a luxurious treat, perfect for a leisurely weekend breakfast or brunch. Enjoy the fluffy texture of the hotcakes complemented by the creamy sweetness of the honeycomb butter!

Avocado and Smoked Trout Bruschetta

Ingredients:

- 1 baguette or Italian bread, sliced into 1/2-inch thick slices
- 2 ripe avocados
- Juice of 1 lemon
- Salt and pepper, to taste
- 150g smoked trout, flaked
- 1 tablespoon capers, drained and chopped
- 2 tablespoons chopped fresh dill
- Extra virgin olive oil, for drizzling
- Optional: Microgreens or arugula for garnish

Instructions:

1. **Prepare the Bread:**
    - Preheat the oven to 375°F (190°C).
    - Arrange the bread slices on a baking sheet in a single layer. Drizzle with olive oil.
    - Bake for 8-10 minutes, or until the bread slices are lightly toasted and crispy. Remove from the oven and set aside.
2. **Prepare the Avocado:**
    - Cut the avocados in half and remove the pits. Scoop the flesh into a bowl.
    - Mash the avocado with a fork until smooth. Add lemon juice, salt, and pepper to taste. Mix well.
3. **Assemble the Bruschetta:**
    - Spread a generous amount of mashed avocado onto each toasted bread slice.
    - Top with flaked smoked trout and chopped capers.
    - Sprinkle with chopped fresh dill.
4. **Serve:**
    - Arrange the Avocado and Smoked Trout Bruschetta on a serving platter.
    - Drizzle with a little extra virgin olive oil.
    - Optionally, garnish with microgreens or arugula for added freshness and color.

Tips:

- **Variations:** You can add thinly sliced red onion, cherry tomatoes, or a sprinkle of red pepper flakes for a bit of heat.
- **Make-Ahead:** Prepare the avocado mixture and toast the bread slices ahead of time. Assemble the bruschetta just before serving to keep the bread crispy.
- **Presentation:** Serve on a wooden board or a decorative platter for an attractive presentation.

Avocado and Smoked Trout Bruschetta is a sophisticated dish that's perfect for entertaining or as a special appetizer. Enjoy the creamy avocado paired with the smoky, savory flavor of the trout on crispy toasted bread!

Dukkah Eggs with Spiced Yogurt

Ingredients:

For the Dukkah:

- 1/2 cup hazelnuts or almonds
- 1/4 cup sesame seeds
- 2 tablespoons coriander seeds
- 2 tablespoons cumin seeds
- 1 tablespoon black peppercorns
- 1 teaspoon sea salt
- 1 teaspoon paprika

For the Spiced Yogurt:

- 1 cup Greek yogurt or labneh
- 1 tablespoon lemon juice
- 1/2 teaspoon ground cumin
- 1/2 teaspoon ground coriander
- Salt and pepper, to taste

For the Eggs:

- 4 large eggs
- 1 tablespoon white vinegar (for poaching)
- Salt and pepper, to taste

Optional Garnishes:

- Fresh herbs (such as cilantro or parsley), chopped
- Extra virgin olive oil
- Toasted bread or pita, for serving

Instructions:

1. **Make the Dukkah:**
    - Toast hazelnuts or almonds in a dry skillet over medium heat until lightly golden and fragrant. Remove from heat and let cool.
    - In the same skillet, toast sesame seeds, coriander seeds, cumin seeds, and black peppercorns until fragrant, about 1-2 minutes. Remove from heat and let cool.

- In a food processor or spice grinder, combine the toasted nuts and seeds with sea salt and paprika. Pulse until coarsely ground. Adjust seasoning to taste.
2. **Prepare the Spiced Yogurt:**
    - In a small bowl, mix together Greek yogurt (or labneh), lemon juice, ground cumin, ground coriander, salt, and pepper. Stir until well combined. Adjust seasoning to taste.
3. **Poach the Eggs:**
    - Fill a large saucepan with water and bring to a simmer over medium heat. Add vinegar (helps to keep the egg whites together).
    - Crack each egg into a small bowl or ramekin.
    - Using a spoon, create a gentle whirlpool in the water to help the egg whites wrap around the yolk. Carefully slide each egg into the simmering water.
    - Poach the eggs for about 3-4 minutes, until the whites are set but the yolks are still runny. Remove with a slotted spoon and drain on a paper towel.
4. **Assemble the Dukkah Eggs:**
    - Spread a generous dollop of spiced yogurt onto each serving plate.
    - Carefully place a poached egg on top of the yogurt.
    - Sprinkle dukkah generously over the eggs and yogurt.
5. **Serve:**
    - Garnish with fresh herbs and drizzle with extra virgin olive oil, if desired.
    - Serve Dukkah Eggs with Spiced Yogurt immediately, accompanied by toasted bread or pita.

Tips:

- **Make-Ahead:** Dukkah can be prepared ahead of time and stored in an airtight container for up to a month. Spiced yogurt can be made a day in advance and kept refrigerated.
- **Variations:** Add a dash of hot sauce or sprinkle of sumac over the eggs for extra flavor.
- **Healthier Option:** Serve with a side of mixed greens or a simple tomato salad for a lighter meal.

Dukkah Eggs with Spiced Yogurt is a delightful dish that combines textures and flavors beautifully, making it perfect for a special breakfast or brunch. Enjoy the contrast of creamy yogurt, crunchy dukkah, and perfectly poached eggs!

www.ingramcontent.com/pod-product-compliance
Lightning Source LLC
LaVergne TN
LVHW081559060526
838201LV00054B/1973